Palgrave Studies in Practice: Global Fashion Brand Management

Branding and internationalization are critical aspects of any business, and the fashion industry is especially global in nature. Very few apparel items are entirely produced within one country, and it is relatively easier for fashion brands to enter international markets because little financial investment is required, small-scale retail space is possible, and economies of scale can be maximized. Accordingly, there are more successful internationalization cases in the fashion industry than any other sector, yet no one text handles these critical topics (i.e., branding and internationalization) in one book, particularly in case study format. This series will focus on fashion brand cases that have been successful in global marketplaces. By examining their strategies in diverse aspects such as internationalization, innovation, branding and communication, and retail management, these books will help students, scholars, and practitioners grasp lesser-known yet effective international marketing strategies.

More information about this series at
http://www.palgrave.com/gp/series/14598

Marta Massi · Alex Turrini
Editors

The Artification of Luxury Fashion Brands

Synergies, Contaminations, and Hybridizations

palgrave
macmillan

Editors
Marta Massi
Desautels Faculty of Management
McGill University
Montréal, Canada

Alex Turrini
Bocconi University
Milan, Italy

Foreword by
Jean-Noël Kapferer
INSEEC U.
Paris, France

ISSN 2523-3505 ISSN 2523-3513 (electronic)
Palgrave Studies in Practice: Global Fashion Brand Management
ISBN 978-3-030-26120-7 ISBN 978-3-030-26121-4 (eBook)
https://doi.org/10.1007/978-3-030-26121-4

This Palgrave Pivot imprint is published by the registered company Springer Nature Switzerland AG
The registered company address is: Gewerbestrasse 11, 6330 Cham, Switzerland

Foreword: The Artification of Luxury—Why Now?

Artification is a relatively new concept, coined only in 2004 by Shapiro and developed jointly by Heinich, the French sociologist. According to these authors, artification refers to a process of transformation, by which that which is not art becomes art. As a process, artification demands major shifts of perspective and vocabulary, such that we no longer talk of production but instead refer to creation; producers become artists; products become artwork; observers become an audience or the public.

The recent emergence of this idea results partly from the expansion of art in postmodern societies: More people engage in symbolic, creative activities than ever, using them as powerful levers to increase the perceived value of goods, objects, and services. Furthermore, hierarchies of perceived personal value within society are no longer simple indicators of accumulated wealth; rather, today they can function as indicators of fame, prestige, creativity, and entrepreneurship, as summarized by the concept of the "creative elite"—terminology coined in 1966 by Weyl. Structurally, these new terms and concepts are symptomatic of the growing recognition of the deep transformation affecting capitalism, producing a new form of aesthetic capitalism (Assouly, 2008) or "Capitalisme artiste" (Lipovetsky & Serroy, 2013).

The recent emergence of artification also resonates with the growing valuation of art. Skyrocketing prices at Sotheby's or Christie's for pieces by contemporary artists offer tangible proof that art has become a gold standard. The world values art, and in turn, many activities get engaged within the process of artification to transform perceptions and social valuations. Accordingly, haute cuisine wants to be recognized as art, not to mention photography, hip hop dancing, the circus, and even luxury—the central focus of this timely and very well-informed book. Yet a question remains unanswered: Why does the luxury sector suddenly need to change public perceptions, through artification? Why now?

In 2014, an influential seminal article on the artification of luxury called attention to the latent, previously unnoticed transformation of luxurybrands' discourse and storytelling, from artisans to artists (Kapferer, 2014). Since that time, the luxury industry increasingly has demanded to be recognized as a fully artistic activity, not an artisanal one. Artisans or craftspeople perform repetitive, hard work, driven by rigor and the need to respect tradition and heritage, two major pillars of value in classic European ideas of luxury. Artists have been distinguished from artisans at least since the sixteenth century, with the assumption that only artists engage in highly conceptual creativity. Yet close, intimate links have always existed between luxury and art. Both share the same public: people with enough money to spend on nonproductive purposes. Both claim to be rare, taking the form of small series for luxury or unique pieces for art. Both claim a sense of eternity, such as when luxury aspires to represent the apex of quality and excellence, and art requires works to pass the barriers of years before they can be called great art.

But some claims might be questionable. For example, is luxury really as rare as its storytelling would suggest? A chasm is evident, between the concept of luxury and the reality of luxury activities. Whereas the concept cites attributes such as unique, rare, exclusive, and prestigious, these terms are remote from the reality of the luxury sector, which has grown steadily for 25 years and is now home to publicly listed conglomerates and megabrands (e.g., LVMH, Kering, EssilorLuxottica, Richemont,

Swatch group, Mercedes Benz) that break records when it comes to competitive advantages and profitability. Managing luxury brands today largely involves creating artificial scarcity, even though the mega-brands have plenty of volume on hand, to cater to the considerable demand of the new riches and upper middle classes from China and other emerging countries. But this reality needs to be hidden, and the story needs to feature rarity.

Consider a significant event that went virtually unnoticed. In 2011, Espace Louis Vuitton (LV) opened in Tokyo, four years before the Parisian version. Why was Tokyo the destination for this first space devoted to contemporary art, under the LV brand umbrella? The answer is that, even before the rise of China, it was Japan that ensured the commercial success of Louis Vuitton. According to one apocryphal story, half of all female office offers in Tokyo once carried a LV handbag. Therefore, to bring back or recreate an aura of exclusivity, the brand chose to ennoble LV, by bestowing the *noblesse* of art!

The brand in turn entered into collaborations with some of the most *avant-garde* artists in the world, with whom it designed limited edition products, in small numbers but priced twice or three times higher. By adopting the codes of art, the brand was able to create links to the creative elites of mature markets and millennials, attracting social media attention to these artful forms of newness. As luxury grows in size and penetration, reaching new layers of the population, questions arise about its social sustainability and legitimacy. Should more people be encouraged to invest huge amounts of money for conspicuous purposes and social representation? If they are eternal, why should people repeatedly buy handbags? To escape the contradiction, many major luxury brands have repositioned themselves and their mission to promote culture, so as to make their commercial aspects less salient.

Jean-Noël Kapferer
INSEEC U.
Paris, France

References

Assouly, O. (2008). *Le Capitalisme esthétique.* Paris: Editions du Cerf.

Kapferer, J.-N. (2014). The artification of luxury, from artisans to artists. *Business Horizons, 57*(3), 371–380.

Lipovetsky, G., & Serroy, J. (2013). *L'Esthétisation du monde.* Paris: Ed.Gallimard.

Shapiro, R. (2004). *What is artification?* Proceedings of the XVII AISLF Conference, Tours, France.

Weyl, N. (1966). *The creative elite in America.* New York: Public Affairs Press.

Jean-Noël Kapferer is an internationally renowned authority on luxury, Ph.D. Kellogg Business School (USA), HEC Paris Emeritus Professor. He now conducts research at INSEEC U. on the mutations of luxury brand management. He is co-author of the reference book *The Luxury Strategy: Break the Rules of Marketing to Build Luxury Brands*, author of *How Luxury Brands Can Grow Yet Remain Rare*, co-editor of *Advances in Luxury Brand Management* and honorary editor of the *Luxury Research Journal.* He leads executive seminars on the challenges impacting luxury, all around the world.

Contents

Notes on Contributors

Federica Antonaglia is a Ph.D. in Entrepreneurship and Innovation from the Department of Strategic Management of the University of Naples 'Luigi Vanvitelli', where she obtained the title of Doctor Europaeus for her international research on museums management in Italy and France. She has extensive experience in teaching management related topics, with a focus on cultural and creative industries. In 2014 she joined the Entrepreneurship Research Team of the IRGO Research center at the University of Bordeaux. Her current research deals with the utility and application of business models in the cultural and creative fields. Recently, she published an article on entrepreneurial orientation in the cultural organizations.

Alessia Anzivino is a post doc at Catholic University of Sacred Heart in Milan, University where she received her Ph.D. in Management. She is researcher at Centrimark (Marketing Research Center) and Professor of Marketing and at the Faculty of Economics of the Catholic University of the Sacred Heart. She also develops research and training activities in collaboration with various universities at national and international level. Her main topics of investigation concern the issues related to the definition of value creation in the management of strategies and business dynamics and issues related to marketing and fundraising of nonprofit organization.

Ariane Berthoin Antal is a Senior Fellow in the Science Policy group at the WZB Berlin Social Science Center, Germany. She is Distinguished Research Professor at Audencia Business School, France and honorary professor at the Technical University of Berlin. Recent books include *Learning Organizations. Extending the Field* (with P. Meusburger & L. Suarsana, Springer, 2014); *Moments of Valuation* (with M. Hutter & D. Stark, OUP, 2015), and *Artistic Interventions in Organizations: Research, Theory and Practice* (with U. Johannson-Sköldberg & J. Woodilla, Routledge, 2016). She has also published extensively on CSR and organizational learning, and presented her findings to policymakers and managers throughout Europe and Asia.

Piergiacomo Mion Dalle Carbonare is a faculty Lecturer at SDA Bocconi School of Management and Ph.D. Candidate in Marketing at the University of Valencia. At SDA Bocconi he coordinates the Master in Arts Management and Administration and he teaches courses on place branding, territorial marketing, and cultural policies. His research interests are mainly in management of cultural institutions. He was a visiting Ph.D. student at SMU Dallas.

Manuel Cuadrado-García is an associate Professor of Marketing at the University of Valencia, Spain. His main research interest is arts marketing—performing arts, music, cinema, and museums—both from a consumer and a managerial perspective. He is engaged in master's and Ph.D. programs in cultural management and marketing in different universities and collaborates with several arts organizations.

Marta Massi, Ph.D. is an assistant Professor of Marketing at Università Cattolica del Sacro Cuore, Milan. She has been a visiting scholar at Deakin University, Australia and McGill University, Canada. Her research interests include country-of-origin, branding and arts and culture marketing. Her work has been published on national and international journals, including *Journal of Consumer Affairs* and *International Journal of Technology Management.*

Chiara Paolino is assistant Professor of Organization theory at Università Cattolica of Milano. Her research interests revolve around individual and organizational learning, innovation, and diversity management. Preferred empirical setting to explore research questions in these fields are creative industries and the space of collaboration between art and corporate logics. Her latest research projects focus on gender discrimination and personal misconduct in the film industry, integration between institutional fields in the setting of TV series production and emotions and innovation process in design companies. Her recent books include *Innovare l'impresa con l'arte* (with Carè and Smarrelli, Egea, 2018) and the forthcoming *Le collezioni corporate in Italia: dalla ricerca alla pratica manageriale* (IlMulino, 2019).

Juliette Passebois Ducros is a French scholar with a Ph.D. in Management Sciences at Montpellier University. She's currently marketing Professor at the Business Administration Institute, University of Bordeaux, France. Her main academic works are dedicated to consumer experiences with artistic products and services and have resulted in publications in international academic journals such as *International Journal of Arts and Management*. She gradually extends her interest to product-oriented industries (wine, luxury …) and the relevance of innovative marketing strategies in this kind of activities. To this end, she is interested in artification strategies and published, in a French review, a paper on artification strategy in luxury wine industry.

Chiara Piancatelli, Ph.D. is a faculty Lecturer at SDA Bocconi School of Management, Milan. Her research activities focus on digital marketing, innovation in communication and marketing and digital transformation. She worked as a visiting research associate at Deakin University, Australia, where she conducted research on the impact of digital technology on consumer behaviour within the arts sector. Chiara works as a research associate at Centrimark at the Cattolica University, Milan.

Stefano Prestini, Ph.D. in Management and Innovation, is an academic Fellow at the Marketing Department at Bocconi University in

Milan, Italy, where he is coordinator of the specialized Master in Marketing and Communication. His current research interests are in consumer behavior, luxury experience, arts marketing, and advertising.

Andrea Rurale, Ph.D. in Marketing at Universidad de Valencia and MsC in Bocconi UNiversity is director of the Master in Arts Management and Administration at SDA Bocconi, Milan and Lecturer in the Marketing Department of Bocconi University. He teaches Heritage Management, Integrated Marketing Communication, Marketing and CRM and Consumer Behavior and Consumer Culture Theory. His current research and interest are in experiential marketing, arts marketing and management, consumer behavior, and luxury experience.

Giorgia Sepe is a consultant in digital transformation. She completed her Ph.D. in Management and Innovation at Università Cattolica del Sacro Cuore, where she worked also as a lecturer and e-teacher. Her research focus is on digital transformation, innovation processes and business-to-business marketing.

Alex Turrini, Ph.D. in Management, Bocconi University, Milan, Italy, is Director of the SMU Meadows Division of Arts Management and Arts Entrepreneurship as well as visiting Professor of arts management and cultural policy at SMU Meadows and Cox School of Business. Tenured as Associate Professor in arts policy and in management at Bocconi University, he carried forward several research, training and consulting projects with different national and international public sector organizations involved in the arts. His research activities center on public policies and management in the arts and cultural sector, arts collecting behavior, and inter-organizational networks in the arts.

List of Figures

List of Tables

1

When Fashion Meets Art: The Artification of Luxury Fashion Brands

Marta Massi and Alex Turrini

"Just a little while ago, as I was crossing the boulevard very hastily and jumping about in the mud, through that moving chaos in which death comes galloping toward you from all sides at once, I moved abruptly and my halo slipped from my head into the mire on the pavement" (Baudelaire 1869)

Abstract This introductory chapter provides the theoretical foundation for the phenomenon of artification—that is, the transformation of nonart into art—which has been increasingly strategically employed by luxury fashion brands in recent times. The chapter provides context and

M. Massi (✉)
Desautels Faculty of Management, McGill University, Montréal, Canada
e-mail: marta.massi@mcgill.ca

A. Turrini
Bocconi University, Milan, Italy
e-mail: aturrini@mail.smu.edu

M. Massi and A. Turrini (eds.), *The Artification of Luxury Fashion Brands*, Palgrave Studies in Practice: Global Fashion Brand Management,
https://doi.org/10.1007/978-3-030-26121-4_1

background to position the case studies analyzed in the following chapters of the book. First, it reviews the literature on artification, tracing the origins of the concept and illustrating its transdisciplinary nature. Second, it lays the groundwork for the identification of the benefits of artification for luxury fashion brands and art institutions. In particular, it illustrates how two apparently far-removed sectors, such as art and luxury fashion, are increasingly interacting and collaborating to achieve mutual benefits. Finally, the chapter proposes a classification of artification processes based on different degrees of interaction between the luxury fashion and art sectors. Notably, the authors identify synergies, contaminations, and hybridizations as incremental stages of the artification of luxury fashion brands.

Keywords Artification · Contaminations · Hybridizations · Luxury fashion brands · Synergies

Introduction

Fashion and art are two distinct systems both socially and economically (Caves, 2000; Geczy & Karaminas, 2012). They have "different modalities of reception [and] presentation" and are "subject to different responses within the economy" (Jelinek, 2018, p. 296). Art fits into the so-called high-culture production field, while fashion is a creativity-based industry (Jelinek, 2018; Steele, 2012a, 2012b). For some scholars, fashion products are mere commodities "with a commercial nature" (Jelinek, 2018, p. 294). For others, fashion is a "form of visual art, a creation of images with the visible self as its medium" (Maynard, 2012; Miller, 2007; Simon, 1995; Wilson, 1987, p. 9). Albeit often perceived as two worlds apart, art and fashion are increasingly converging in mutually advantageous ways, especially when it comes to luxury, one of the fastest-growing sectors: in 2018, the market for personal luxury goods was €260 billion, with a growth of 6% (Bain & Company, 2018).

This book deals with the artification of luxury fashion brands, that is, their transformation into art (Kapferer, 2014, p. 371). Having been hotly debated lately, the phenomenon of artification has attracted both the praise of those who see in it an opportunity to purify luxury goods from their long-stigmatized link to unnecessary excess and amorality (Dubois, Laurent, & Czellar, 2001; Kapferer, 2014) and the criticism of those who view it as a desecration of art. Despite strong criticism, mainly based on the assumption that artification is instrumental only for achieving marketing and sales goals (to the detriment of artistic integrity), there are many upsides to artification processes in the context of luxury fashion brands.

The overall purpose of this book is to explore the ways in which the luxury fashion industry and the art world might join forces, both strengthening the luxury brand reputation and supporting the flourishing of the arts and the economic sustainability of nonprofit arts organizations. In particular, the authors aim to delve into the synergies, contaminations, and hybridizations between luxury fashion brands and art. This book investigates such phenomena by presenting different case studies of fashion businesses "artifying" their brands by establishing various types of interactions with the art world.

In this chapter, we propose an overall framework distinguishing among several levels of artification processes in the luxury fashion industry. The chapter is organized as follows. First, we review the concept of artification, illustrating its multidisciplinary nature and highlighting the mutual benefits for luxury fashion companies and art organizations that engage in artification processes. Second, we propose a classification of artification processes based on different degrees of interaction between the luxury fashion and art sectors. In particular, we identify synergies, contaminations, and hybridizations as incremental stages of the artification process.

The Concept of Artification

Albeit apparently recalling a negative or derogatory meaning—mainly for its association to the idea of the "fabrication of what is artificial" and as "commoditization, destructive of the authenticity of things"[1]—the

[1] «L'artification serait la fabrication de l'artificiel, entendue comme une opération peu glorieuse de marchandisation, destructrice de l'authenticité des choses».

term "artification" must be employed in mere descriptive terms (Shapiro, 2004a, p. 1). In her seminal article, Shapiro describes artification as "the transformation of non-art into art [that is] a transfiguration of people, objects and action" (Shapiro, 2004a, p. 1).[2]

Artification can be read as a consequence of "a general objectification of culture occurring in many societies" (Shapiro, 2004b, p. 2) and of the blurring between high and low culture characterizing the so-called "culture society" (Morato, 2003; Shapiro, 2004b), where the boundaries of art are not well-defined (Shapiro, 2004b). As Shapiro (2004b, pp. 2–3) puts it, there are two basic assumptions on which the artification concept is based: (1) the belief in the superior value of artworks, conceived as outcomes of a process rather than as objects. Artification does not deal with the intrinsic nature of art but with the activity through which art is generated (Heinich & Shapiro, 2012b); and (2) the multiplication of legitimizing bodies. Once, legitimation was the prerogative of a few privileged bodies (e.g., the Academy of France) who used to discern what held artistic value and what did not. In contrast, the power to legitimate an object has now become the right of multiple legitimating bodies, including the audience, newspapers, collectors, gallery or festival directors, sponsors, etc. (Shapiro, 2004b, pp. 2–3).

Therefore, artification can be regarded as a consequence of the cultural democratization characterizing the postmodern era (Shapiro, 2004b), which allows for "countless possibilities in the world of art and architecture" (Firat & Venkatesh, 1995, p. 242), also giving those who were once considered outsiders and marginalized groups a chance to enter the art world. Thanks to artification, genres such as breakdance, hip pop, video art, and computer art acquired artistic dignity and value (Shapiro, 2004b).

Rooted in many fields and allowing for multiple levels of analysis, artification dynamics have been studied by different disciplines. From a biological stance, artification is the individual attempt to assure the survival and evolution of the species (Dissanayake, 2011) From a sociological standpoint, artification is used by individuals to achieve the right to self-expression and authenticity (Shapiro & Heinrich, 2012) From

---

[2]«Bref, la transformation du non-art en art est une transfiguration des personnes, des objets et de l'action».

a socioeconomic viewpoint, artification is the consequence of the individual's reaction to crucial changes occurring in important institutions (i.e., family, workplace, etc.) and an attempt of individuals to use art to restore their identity (DiMaggio, 1982). Politically, artification is a consequence of democratization processes occurring at the cultural level (Erjavec, 2012). From the art history perspective, artification allows for rewriting the history of art by including new styles and genres (Shapiro, 2004b).

In addition to being studied in different disciplines, artification is a process occurring in different fields. Artification processes are emerging outside the field of luxury fashion, including in the leisure and tourism, entertainment, sports, and technology fields (Heinich & Shapiro, 2012b). The development of the artification concept by Shapiro (2004b) and Shapiro and Heinich (2012) does not come without criticism. Creux (2012) contested this conceptualization of artification, stating that Shapiro and Heinich (2012) simply described a process of artistic legitimization without further explaining how an object or a practice can become artified. For Creux (2012), the proposed concept of artification emerges as "forced" and does not offer "a means of complementary comprehension of the process of the transition to art."[3] Heinich & Shapiro (2012a) replied that their interpretation of the concept is more sophisticated than what is stated by Creux. For the authors, legitimization addresses a hierarchical issue, defining the border between what is superordinate and what is subordinate. In contrast, artification addresses an ontological question, defining the border between what is defined as art and what is not. Under this perspective, legitimation is a "paradigm of evaluation" and does not lead—as artification does—to the construction of a world through "material, organizational, formal transformations" (Heinich & Shapiro, 2012a). As such, the concept of artification implies some degree of a sector's change and reorganization. As will be shown in the next sections, this phenomenon is particularly evident in the field of luxury fashion brands.

[3]«Un outil de compréhension complémentaire au processus du passage à l'art».

The Artification Process

As previously mentioned, artification is inherently processual: it is "a dynamic process of social change through which new objects and practices emerge and relationships and institutions are transformed" (Shapiro & Heinich, 2012, p. 2). Through artification, an object changes its status and goes through a transformation that results in that object being socially accepted and, therefore, legitimated. According to Shapiro and Heinich (2012) and Shapiro (2019), artification involves a number of subprocesses, namely, (1) displacement, (2) renaming, (3) recategorization, (4) institutional and organizational change, (5) the differentiation of functions, (6) normative and legal consolidation, (7) the redefinition of time, (8) aesthetic formalization, (9) patronage, and (10) intellectualization.

1. *Displacement*: To be artified, an object must be taken out of the contexts it belongs to. In this way, it can be circulated, "transformed, and exchanged" (Shapiro, 2019, p. 267). The blurring between high and low culture contributes to displacing objects from their environment of origin. This phenomenon has been observed for various products, including films, jazz, and graffiti: "when paintings shifted from frescoes to the easel in 14th-century Italy, when graffiti was photographed and published in books, when jazz was first transcribed into musical notation, when film broke away from its initial site at fairs, or when breakdancers stepped off the streets to go on stage" (Shapiro, 2019, pp. 267–268). Similarly, in the fashion sector, it is increasingly more common to view products that are displayed in museums and exhibition spaces or pictured in arts magazines as artworks. As a result, fashion has become "a form of cultural heritage" and acquired "artistic value" (Crane, as cited in Shapiro, 2019, p. 268).
2. *Renaming*: Otherwise known as the terminological changes that occur as a consequence of displacement (Shapiro, 2019), renaming is also particularly evident in the context of luxury fashion brands, where products such as clothes are increasingly regarded as artworks (e.g., the Louis Vuitton bag designed by Murakami). Moreover,

charismatic designers in particular are "starified" and regarded as artists, for example, John Galliano and Alexander McQuinn (Dion & Arnould, 2011; Kapferer, 2012; Passebois-Ducros, Trinquecoste, & Pichon, 2015). Some DJs producing music through sampling are called composers-performers (Shapiro, 2004a). Through renaming, the "metteur en scène" (theater director) becomes the "regisseur" (manager), making it possible for these professionals to be regarded as artists (Proust cited in Shapiro, 2019, p. 268). Similarly, "dress-making" becomes "haute couture," thus providing the category with more prestige (Shapiro, 2019, p. 268).

3. *Recategorization*: Includes "reshuffling rankings" that comes with renaming (Shapiro, 2019, p. 268; Shapiro & Heinich, 2012) whereby what was once addressed as a mere product is now regarded as an art object. The evolution of breakdancing is exemplary: from "disorderly conduct" (Banes, 1994) to professional endeavor (Shapiro, 2012).
4. *Institutional and organizational change*: Is the main consequence of recategorization (Shapiro, 2019). For instance, the emergence of big fashion corporations led to organizational changes in the sector (Shapiro, 2019). At the same time, the institutionalization of artified objects comes with legitimization (DiMaggio, 1988). For instance, the musical genre of rap originated from the "underworld of esthetic respectability" (Shusterman, 1991, p. 613) and reached artistic status. Similarly, hip-hop dance shifted from being the expression of a specific social group to representing a genre that can be integrated into the repertory of contemporary dance (Shapiro, 2004a).
5. *Differentiation of functions*: Is a consequence of change and occurs with some positions becoming preeminent. Similar to what occurs in the art field when orchestra conductors superseded musicians or choreographers superseded dancers, luxury fashion couturiers are now shadowing tailors (Shapiro, 2019).
6. *Normative and legal consolidation*: This represents the next step in the artification process that leads to changes in the legalities of artworks, for instance, the recognition of writers' and composers' intellectual property rights in the nineteenth century.

7. *The redefinition of time*: Artification processes also affect *time definition.* What was originally an improvised show (e.g., breakdance) must now be coherently structured and organized to follow new norms (Shapiro & Heinich, 2012).
8. *Aesthetic formalization*: Artified objects become aesthetically formalized and start following the rules of already established arts (e.g., fashion designers that apply the rules of visual art) (Shapiro, 2019).
9. *Patronage*: Once an object has been artified, public subsidies and government endowments become available, sanctioning "an ontological difference between art and other activities deemed unworthy of such official monies" (Shapiro, 2019, p. 271). In this sense, artification corresponds to a process of legitimation.
10. *Intellectualization*: The last step of the artification process includes *discursive reinforcement and the intellectualization of practice* (Shapiro & Heinich, 2012, p. 5). The production of discourse around an object (media discourse, art critique, etc.) contributes to ratifying its artification (Shapiro, 2019).

Artification in the Luxury Fashion Industry

Artification occurs in the luxury fashion industry, as luxury fashion and art have many commonalities. First, luxury products are characterized by excellent quality, very high price, scarcity and uniqueness, aesthetics and polysensuality, ancestral heritage, and superfluousness (Dubois et al., 2001; Jin & Cedrola, 2016, 2017). All these features are also shared by art objects, therefore making both artworks and luxury fashion costly creations that "aim at the same target: the cultural elite" (Kapferer, 2014, p. 375).

Second, art and luxury are "independent of function" (Kapferer, 2014, p. 375): both luxury and art consumers are driven to satisfy a need that is far from functional. As specialty goods, luxury and art do not function to satisfy fundamental needs such as hunger and thirst. In contrast, they are meant to satisfy aesthetic or symbolic needs (Park, Jaworski, & MacInnis, 1986). Fashion products are sought by consumers aiming to demonstrate individual self-esteem, personality, and social status (Banister & Hogg,

2004; Tarrant & Jolles, 2012). Consumers of fashion products are usually motivated by identity building and expression and the intention to impress others (Phau & Siew Leng, 2008; Piacentini & Mailer, 2004). Since the symbolic value takes precedence over the functional value, both art and luxury are meant to be for eternity or at least for "timelessness" (Kapferer, 2014, p. 375). In addition, independence of function implies that price and function are not correlated (Kapferer, 2014), as the price of luxury products, which by definition are exclusive (Dubois et al., 2001), is determined by criteria other than their function.

For all these reasons, art and luxury are progressively getting closer to the point where art is defined as "the cornerstone of luxury brands" (Soito, 2018). At the same time, to maintain the perceived uniqueness and exclusivity of their products, luxury companies adopt unconventional and counterintuitive business models based on real "anti-laws of marketing" and resembling arts organizations like opera houses or visual art dealers (Kapferer, 2012, p. 456; Kapferer & Bastien, 2009). Indeed, they tend to keep full control of the value chain, especially controlling production (which is not delocalized) and distribution (that does not contemplate licensing) (Kapferer, 2014, p. 456). In terms of the marketing mix, luxury companies tend to emphasize their products, which are unique and exclusive, rather than invest in advertising. Instead, such companies prefer adopting communication strategies such as product placement and one-to-one marketing. In addition, they continually raise the average price of their products (Kapferer, 2014, p. 456), as price is the main signal of exclusivity. In addition, by promoting their products as a form of art and presenting their designers as artists, fashion businesses can provide their brands with an allure of authenticity, uniqueness, rarity and scarcity, that is, features that seem to get lost, owing to the industrial production of many of these goods and the counterfeiting phenomenon. Examples of artist–brand alliances abound in the fashion sector, both in the luxury (e.g., Takashi Murakami for Louis Vuitton) and in the fast-fashion market (e.g., Jeff Koons for H&M) (Atwood, 2014; Kim, Chang, Vaidyanathan, & Stoel, 2018). Yves Saint Laurent clothes that reproduce Mondrian, Picasso, or Trussardi and that cite Caravaggio are but a few examples of fashion brands' attempts to become immortal (Baumgarth, 2018).

As will be evident in the following chapters, the artification of luxury fashion companies is evidenced by other strategic moves. With increasing frequency, luxury fashion companies are creating their foundations or museums (Kubler & Smith, 2013) to gain legitimacy and authenticity in the eyes of consumers and society at large. By establishing museums and foundations that carry the same brand name (e.g., the Fondazione Trussardi and the Gucci Museum), inaugurating art exhibitions, or supporting artists, luxury fashion firms gain a legitimate role in society as they promote arts and culture as well as the public institutions, thus promoting their Corporate Social Responsibility (CRS) (Kottasz, Bennet, Savani, & Ali-Choudhury, 2008).

On top of these trends in the context of luxury fashion, artification has been evident in branding. In this particular domain, artification has consisted of "a transformation of non-art into art ... that requires the active collaboration of art authorities and renowned artists" aimed to "change the status of the brand, of its founder and products, and in so doing, to reinforce the idea of a better-than ordinary brand whose price and symbolic power are undisputed" (Kapferer, 2014, p. 371).

Recently, artification phenomena and the blending of brands and art (Codignola & Rancati, 2016) in the luxury field have become so pervasive and frequent that some introduced the term "art-keting," a neologism that describes the collaboration between marketing and the art world (Passebois-Ducros et al., 2015). In fact, the luxury sector and, specifically, the luxury fashion industry can greatly benefit from the artification of brands. Some of the advantages of artification include the following:

Legitimacy: The institutional theory of organizations posits that organizations must conform to ceremonial rules and norms to become legitimate in their environment (Meyer & Rowan, 1977). By getting closer to and collaborating with the arts, luxury fashion brands can prove their adherence to a cultural genre or superordinate system (DiMaggio, 1988), thus becoming legitimate in the eyes of consumers. Luxury fashion brands can benefit from the legitimacy provided to them by their link to art. As a field with a universally recognized social role, art can provide fashion firms with the legitimizing dignity they need to exist and survive in a competitive environment. From an ethical point of view, luxury has been historically condemned (Kapferer, 2014) and is often regarded as a symbol of moral corruption. Marie Antoinette, the last Queen of France, who used to indulge in a very luxurious lifestyle, has often been portrayed as an example of corruption and debauchery.

In addition, the fashion world has been downplayed many times by critics who never recognized fashion products' equivalence to artworks, mainly because "fashion designers have never managed to gain total recognition as artists" (Weissman, 1967). Long considered to be the reign of excess and surplus, luxury is, therefore, increasingly becoming "artified" (Baumgarth, Lohrisch, & Kastner, 2014; Kapferer, 2014) to become legitimate and authentic and differentiate themselves by defining a unique and exclusive identity. Art provides fashion brands with "an aesthetic and moral endorsement" and the "legitimation of its extraordinary prices" (Jelinek, 2018, p. 296). In other words, art can wash away the sins associated with the very essence of luxury, providing a "moral and aesthetic endorsement, non-commercial connotations and a paradoxical legitimation of its high prices" (Kapferer, 2014, p. 375).

Authenticity: The concept of legitimacy, as defined in institutional theory, is similar to that of authenticity (Massi, 2020) because it assumes the existence of legitimating bodies (DiMaggio, 1988) or institutions that confer legitimacy, such as the critics that assess the originality of artworks. Developed in the museum context, the notion of authenticity not only refers to the certification of an artwork's authorship but also refers to being "true to oneself," broadly speaking (Trilling, 1972). Authenticity as "truth to oneself" is especially crucial for luxury fashion brands (Carù, Ostillio, & Leone, 2017). To be regarded as authentic and therefore legitimate, luxury fashion brands must be perceived as "disinterested" and "disseminated by parties without an instrumental economic agenda" (Holt, 2002, p. 83). By being artified, luxury fashion brands gain the "aura" of the art world (Kim, 1998; Steele, 2012a). By getting closer to art, luxury fashion companies can manage to position their "products as authentic pieces of contemporary art, each one blessed by the hand of the designer" (Kapferer, 2012, p. 458). Further, customization and the artist's signature make it possible to turn "their limited editions into authentic artworks" (Kapferer, 2014, p. 376).

Expertise and artisanality: One of the main challenges posed by industrial production is that of preserving the idea of artisanality behind the manufacture of luxury goods. The logic of production volumes seems to have superseded that of craftsmanship, "which requires time and effort" (Kapferer, 2014, p. 458). In times of mechanical and digital reproduction (Benjamin, 2008), when infinite copies can be produced from an original prototype (e.g., counterfeited goods) (Nia & Zaichkowsky, 2000), luxury fashion brands use artification strategies to stress the importance of traditional handcrafted and artisanal methods and intuitive expertise to create a sense of authenticity (Beverland, 2005; Kapferer, 2014). The latest advertising campaign from Dolce & Gabbana, "Fatto a mano" (handmade) is just one of the examples of the companies that emphasize their artisanal dimension.

Uniqueness and Exclusivity: Modern consumers are no longer willing to accept price as the only signal of a good's uniqueness (Codignola & Rancati, 2016). Maintaining exclusivity is currently one of the biggest challenges for luxury firms, as it is incompatible with the logics of volumes and market expansion (Kapferer, 2012). One of the corollaries of the preservation of the idea of artisanship is that luxury fashion companies present and promote their products as a form of art, thus providing their brands with an allure of uniqueness. In addition, by reinforcing the idea of distance and separation from what is a unique object and its copies, luxury fashion companies manage to exclusively target the cultural elite (Kapferer, 2014).

Aesthetics/emotional experiences: Intangible benefits are more preeminent for luxury brands than for ordinary brands (Koronaki, Kyrousi, & Panigyrakis, 2018), since individuals employ these brands as symbols to define their identity. Artification can greatly help stress the aesthetic and emotional dimensions of the luxury brands that consumers of luxury goods pursue. For instance, Koronaki et al. (2018) found that arts-based initiatives have an emotional value for consumers which, in turn, can lead to increased loyalty toward the brand. In this sense, artification allows for providing "emotional experiences," which are highly valued by customers (Batat, 2019, p. 136).

Scarcity and rarity: Being handcrafted, artworks are also scarce and rare as opposed to commodified and mass-produced. The scarcity effect is a rule in the luxury sector. For instance, luxury wine companies, such as Romanée-Conti, produce only a few thousand bottles of wine per year. Companies such as Ferrari and Patek Philippe restrict their production. In the luxury sector, as soon as a product's sales increase, production is discontinued. In the words of Hermes' CEO, "When a product sells too much we stop producing it" (Kapferer & Bastien, 2012, p. 70). A typical example of goods that have maintained their aura of scarcity and rarity over years is the Birkin bag from Hermes. To purchase it, it is not sufficient to be able to afford it; rather, it is necessary to be included on a very exclusive customer list, and the wait can last for years.

Aura: Associated with the aura (halo) concept is that of sacredness, a characteristic of artworks. In ancient times, art and luxury shared the same places of worship (temples, churches, pagodas, and pyramids) (Kapferer, 2012, p. 454). As Kapferer (2014, p. 371) observes, "the popularization/overuse of the word 'luxury' blurs distinctions and creates managerial confusion." As the poet referred to by Baudelaire in the famous poem "Loss of Halo" (Perte d'Aureole), luxury has lost the aura that marked its sacredness. Artification can allow luxury fashion companies to win back their aura of sacredness.

Thus, luxury fashion brands can greatly benefit from art's social, cultural, and symbolic capital (Rodner & Kerrigan, 2014). In pragmatic terms, luxury fashion businesses can benefit from collaboration with the arts by enhancing their corporate reputation and image (McNicholas, 2004; Schwaiger, Sarstedt, & Taylor, 2010; Quester & Thompson, 2001), increasing their consumer purchase intention and customer loyalty (Carrillat, D'astous, & Colbert, 2008; Mermiri, 2010), entering new markets, and extending their brands (Hagtvedt & Patrick, 2008a; Kapferer, 2014).

For all these reasons, luxury fashion brands are increasingly employing art strategically. As a consequence, novel paradigms such as "luxury is art" (Okonkwo, 2009), "art strategy" (Kapferer, 2014), and the "M(Art) World" (Joy, Wang, Chan, Sherry, & Cui, 2014) are emerging in the fashion sector.

Artification has been studied in the context of luxury wines (Passebois-Ducros et al., 2015) and luxury fashion (Kapferer, 2014); however, research on the phenomenon is still in its infancy. Surprisingly, there is a dearth of research on the interactions between art and fashion, and particularly on the implementation of art in luxury fashion brands (Baumgarth et al., 2014; Jelinek, 2018; Kubler & Smith, 2013; Sjöholm & Pasquinelli, 2014; Teunissen, 2009), with few academic studies on the topic (e.g., Joy et al., 2014; Kastner, 2013). In the following, we identify and classify the artification strategies of luxury fashion companies, laying the groundwork for future research and studies on this topic.

Artification and the Levels of Collaboration Between Art and Luxury Fashion

As previously mentioned, we aim at providing a categorization of the artification strategies that luxury fashion firms employ when they join the art world. Building on Kapferer (2015), we developed a continuum (Fig. 1.1) illustrating how luxury fashion companies and the arts' world can interact at different levels. On one end of the continuum are the *synergies*, that is, the collaborations to achieve common goals (for example, sponsorships), which represent an initial point of contact between the two. Unlike *contaminations* (e.g., corporate museums), which represent the next level of the continuum, synergies do not affect (or contaminate) the respective natures of luxury fashion brands and art. On the other end are *hybridizations*, which imply the overlapping of forms and genres (e.g., a fashion object that becomes an artwork). In the following sections, the synergies, contaminations, and hybridizations are presented and described through examples.

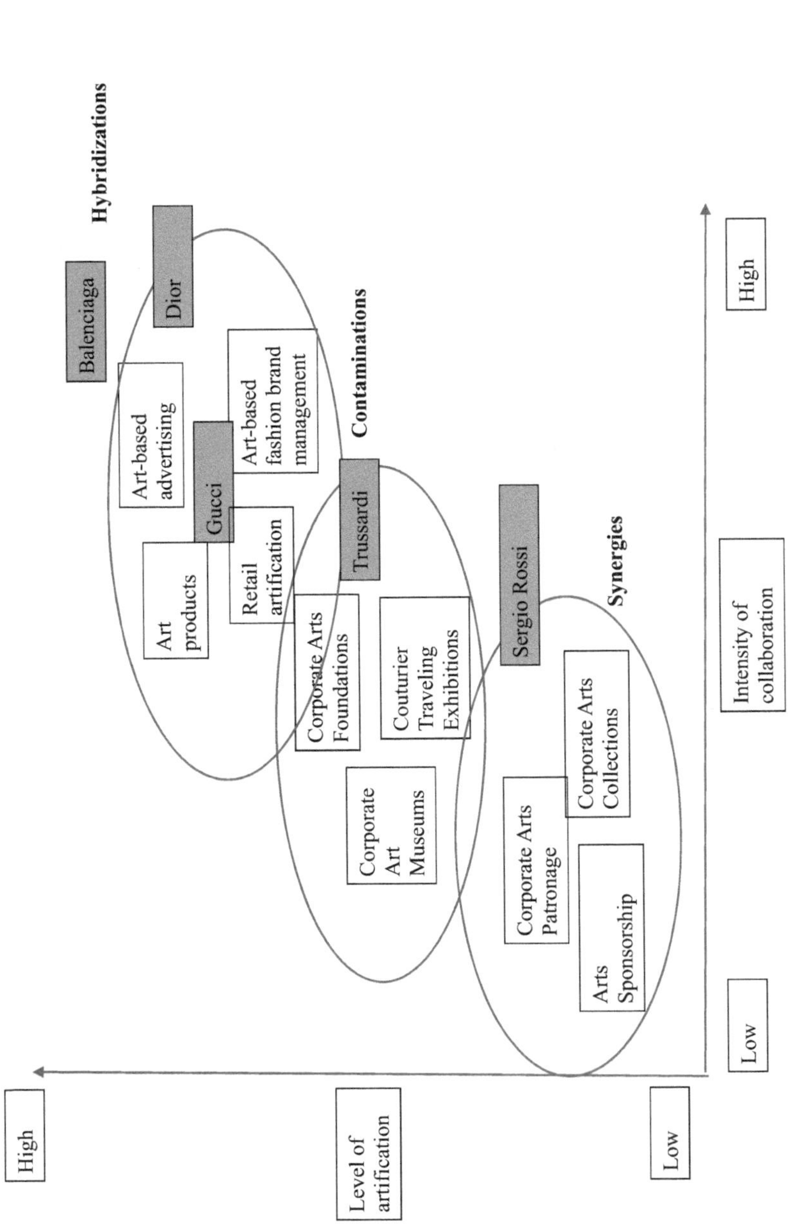

Fig. 1.1 Levels of artification

Synergies

Synergies are intended as collaborations that are built to achieve different goals and do not radically affect (or contaminate) the nature of either the luxury fashion company/brand or the arts institution involved. Among these types of collaboration, we might include the following:

Sponsorship. Sponsorship implies a *do ut des* relationship between sponsors and sponsees: it is characterized by a relationship that envisages some form of promotion, even if only in terms of image that the company receives in exchange for its support of an artist, a cultural activity, or a cultural institution. Sponsorship, in fact, is a commercial agreement, according to which an organization financially supports a second part in exchange for direct or indirect benefits (Worth, 2016). Above all in Europe, sponsorships for the renovation or restoration of historic buildings or the organization of exhibitions or awards for young talents have been the main actions in the artistic-cultural field by fashion companies. The choice of the single initiative usually responds to a specific investment strategy, in line with the company objectives and values (Finkel, 2010). An example includes the "FENDI for Fountains" project launched in 2013 to finance the restoration of the Quattro Fontane and the Trevi Fountain in Rome. Another renowned example is the sponsorship of Diego Della Valle, the Chairman of Tod's, who has been involved in "a five-year project that cost the brand over €25 million" to fund renovations of the Colosseum in Rome (Chen, 2016). In return, Tod's was allowed to use the Colosseum logo in their communications. Another company that has engaged in synergies with the art world is Bulgari, which was involved in the refurbishment of Rome's Baths of Caracalla and the Spanish Steps (Chen, 2016). Despite some criticisms, according to which creativity cannot be subject to market rules, it must be recognized that sponsorship is usually advantageous, not only for the company, but also for the sponsored artist/institution. Moreover, companies are increasingly moving away from the logic of mere monetary transactions in exchange for the presence of their logo on promotional material, to search for collaboration models that involve a higher degree of involvement with the artist or sponsored institution. This encompasses the definition of shared project objectives, up to a common vision of what the expected benefits could be (Mermiri, 2010). In this sense, sponsorship more frequently assumes the connotations of a partnership between the corporate fashion world and the art world. These new forms of cooperation imply a convergence of values recognized by both partners, a high level of synergy in the implementation of the project and objectives that goes beyond simple marketing or fundraising.

Arts Patronage. The concept of patronage has very ancient historical origins and, undoubtedly, its connection to generosity and gratuitousness has remained unchanged. For a long time the prerogative of political power, the Church, and wealthy private individuals who offered money and hospitality to artists in exchange for commissioned works, patronage has spread within the corporate culture only in recent times. It flourished especially in England and in the United States of the twenties, due to the desire of corporations and CEOs to show their economic and financial power. Support for local artists has been widely regarded as a form of active citizenship or commitment to the community. By financing national artists, companies were and are able to improve their image and strengthen their corporate identity (Alexander, 1996). However, we must not forget how, in many other situations, the commission of works and liberal donations derives from an authentic passion for the art of top management and property and from their desire to return, at least in part, to the territory and community of reference, what they have given to the company. Given its characteristics, patronage is very often part of broader programs of corporate social responsibility, which embrace ethics, the environment, and human capital (Comunian, 2009). As a matter of fact, patronage is often associated with actions such as:

- *Awards*, which might be set up with the aim of directly supporting artists or of promoting beauty and creativity. One of the most famous awards in the luxury sector is the Montblanc de la Culture Arts Patronage Award, an internationally renowned award founded in

1992 that is bestowed every year to "outstanding private patrons of the arts throughout the world" (Montblanc, 2020).

- *Artistic mentoring*, an ad hoc program for emerging and young artists to support their work and help them emerge in the market. An example is the Mentor and Protégé Arts Initiative launched by Rolex in 2002 to support artists in the fields of architecture, cinema, music, literature, or other forms of creativity (Rolex, 2020).
- *Workshops, conventions, and seminars* which, in some cases, might see the participation of representatives of the arts world and the business community.
- *The stipulation of barter agreements*, according to which a company supports one or more artists in exchange for their presence at company events or the designing of certain products.
- *The implementation of editorial projects*, which might include books describing the company's history, photographic books that tell about corporate collaborations with the art world, and catalogs of sponsored exhibitions, as well as video installations curated by artists, with the aim of contributing to the corporate storytelling.

Corporate art collections, the first of which was created in the early twentieth-century United States, though it was only after the Second World War that the phenomenon was fully developed (Martorella, 1990). In the fifties, in fact, the great American multinationals complemented the commission of advertising campaigns to famous designers and artists with reserving spaces to exhibit certain works, which were the expression of an emerging artistic movements era. In most cases, it was the property and the top management that created the first nucleus of the collection, thanks to their proximity and personal contacts with artists or arts dealers and their passion for collecting. The works collected were to be considered an asset also in terms of corporate communication despite the fact that these collections were not originally accessible, having as their first function to demonstrate the company's power and economic-financial solidity to customers and suppliers (Wu, 2002). More recently, collections have been opened to the public (Kottasz et al., 2008; Paolino, Bissola, & Imperatori, 2018) or have been used as vehicles to beautify office spaces and improve organizational well-being (LeClair

& Doornbosch, 1995; Paolino, 2019). Finally, corporate collections have been considered sets of tangible asset capable of increasing the company's market value or of being marketed "at the right time" to make a profit (Ardenne, 1995).

Contaminations

In the middle of the continuum, *contaminations* occur when art and fashion companies meet at a deeper level than with synergies but do not give up their specific natures. Through contamination effects, art's key properties spill over onto brands, thus influencing consumer evaluation (Chu, Jung, & Kim, 2010; Estes, Brotto, & Busacca, 2018; Hagtvedt & Patrick, 2008a, 2008b). Contaminations are types of collaborations where an art infusion effect is occurring on fashion luxury companies (Hagtvedt & Patrick, 2008a; Kim et al., 2012; Lee & Han, 2010, 2011; Naletelich & Paswan, 2018; Peluso, Pino, Amatulli, & Guido, 2017). At this stage, artification benefits luxury companies as they upgrade their brand-infusing characteristics such as rarity and value (Chailan, 2018; Chailan & Valek, 2014), prestige (Lee, Chen, & Wang, 2015), and legitimacy (Hagtvedt & Patrick, 2008a) into fashion products and brands. Contamination effects are mutual: fashion brands can, indeed, contaminate art, for example, when artists are invited to create works of art from luxury products (Dion & Arnould, 2011). We might include in this category those actions developed by fashion companies that include a deeper commitment toward the arts, such as:

Corporate (art) museums: Corporate collecting must not only be conceived from a strictly artistic point of view. In fact, even before beginning to collect works of art, fashion companies have begun to preserve memorabilia, such as industrial designs, prototypes, machinery, and other materials related to their activity. The main functions of these special collections range from the desire to transmit and spread the corporate culture, to the possibility of strengthening the bond with employees, and the ability to tell a story through a set of objects, building a collective memory, as well as the opportunity to draw inspiration from the past to generate new ideas and solutions for the future. The objects collected are often displayed in such a way as to tell the visitor the evolution of the company's history, the materialization of the creative process, and the relationships with the various people and the different knowledges that have contributed to the company's success over the years (Bargenda, 2019). Corporate museums in the fashion industry play two roles: on one hand, they become a reference point for the future accumulation of artworks (Vacca, 2014) and, on the other hand, they strengthen the company's presence in the artistic or cultural field. Therefore, a corporate museum functions as a company's historical archive and represents a dynamic space that hosts a permanent collection, temporary exhibitions (often by contemporary artists), and educational workshops on different themes aimed at students of diverse grades and ages.

Art foundations: Very often, corporate museums are managed directly by the company; in other cases instead, a foundation is set up with the aim of administering the company's artistic heritage and financing actions in support of its culture. In other cases, there is a combination of these two legal frameworks. Many are the companies that have their own foundations for developing artistic projects (e.g., Louis Vuitton, Cartier, Prada, and Trussardi [which is the subject of Chapter 3 of this book]). The constitution of a foundation or fund is often conceived as a tool to prevent the dispersion of the corporate cultural heritage in the event of a financial crisis, and is therefore increasingly adopted both in Europe and in Asia, where art programs are generally structured with a long-term vision. Having a governance that is distinct from that of the company makes collaboration with other cultural institutions and the possible exposure of artworks to the public much easier. The selection of the works or initiatives to be supported is very often entrusted to a select committee, which includes some members of the board of directors and a curator who usually reports to the managing director. Art foundations play a crucial role in the artification process, as they not only represent the means for celebrating the brand but also contribute to developing the relationship between the brand and the territory.

Exhibitions: The Armani exhibit at the Guggenheim Museum in 2000 represents a great example of a successful collaboration between art and fashion, which created many contrasts among the Guggenheim Museum Board members. At the same time, luxury fashion firms are eager to bring art into their stores, turning their stores into exhibition spaces where customers can admire artworks along with the products (e.g., Gucci) (Lipovetsky & Manlow, 2009). Such closeness between fashion products and artworks can trigger win-win collaboration processes. Other famous examples include the Culture Chanel exhibit at the National Art Museum of China a Pechino in 2011 and the Christian Dior exhibit at the Victoria & Albert Museum in London in 2019.

Hybridizations

Hybridizations are collaborations characterized by an extreme level of interaction that implies the intersection of forms and genres, generating grafts between high culture and commercial culture (e.g., the Vuitton bag designed by Murakami). Through hybridization, fashion items—designed by artists—become real works of art. Luxury fashion companies involve artists in designing special capsules or limited editions of their products. In this way, artification allows for turning an elitist—but still commercial product—into a hybrid that acquires aesthetic and symbolic value and reclaims the aura lost due to production logics. Balenciaga and Dior, whose Haute Couture products are often regarded as art (Jelinek, 2018) since contemporary artists are involved in the creation project, are exemplary instances of hybridization processes. Hybridization has made it possible to elevate fashion designers such as Marc Jacobs of Louis Vuitton and Miuccia Prada "to the role of insightful intellectuals" (Tokatli, 2014, p. 6). Artification strategies based on hybridization can be employed "at different levels of brand strategy: from communication to product design to retail sites" (Vukadin, Wongkitrungrueng, & Assarut, 2018, p. 278). Specifically, hybridization can take on different forms, including:

- *Art products*: Many fashion companies have collaborated with artists to develop iconic capsule collections or limited editions. Examples include Yves Saint Laurent, with the "Mondrian Collection;" John Galliano, who honored Gustav Klimt, reinterpreting his most important works for Dior's 2008 spring collection; and Elsa Schiaparelli, who worked with Salvador Dalí to develop one of her most famous designs, the lobster dress. One of the pioneers in this field is certainly Louis Vuitton, who collaborated with artists such as Takashi Murakami, Richard Prince, Yayoi Kusama, and Stephen Sprouse, making an "aesthetic investment in the immaterial and symbolic definition of the brand" (Crewe, 2016, p. 8). Another example is the collaboration between Alexander McQueen and Damien Hirst, who created a limited edition of what is now the iconic skull print scarf (Moncayo, 2019).
- *Retail artification*: Defined as "a new form of spatial aesthetics" (Vukadin et al., 2018, p. 279), retail artification can help redefine a store's atmospherics, introducing new opportunities for customer engagement. Such initiatives can include: (1) the in-store display of permanent or temporary artworks such as paintings, sculptures, and/or installations; (2) the presence of artistic elements in the store's architecture and interior design; and (3) the organization of live performance art events (Godey, Lagier, & Pederzoli, 2009; Vukadin et al., 2018, p. 280). Again, the pioneer in this field was Louis Vuitton, whose creative director Marc Jacobs collaborated with artist Olafur Eliasson in 2006 to develop The Eye See You, "a site-specific store installation that challenges the tropes of retail design and display and actively enrolled the consumer in the production and interpretation of the space—visuality at its most stark" (Crewe, 2016, p. 9). Research that investigated the effects of stores' artification on consumers (e.g., Joy et al., 2014; Vukadin, Lemoine, & Badot, 2016; Vukadin et al., 2018) identified the positive effects of artification on consumer perceptions (e.g., on customer-perceived value) (Vukadin et al., 2018).
- *Art-based brand management*: Interactions between art and branding are a sign of the postmodern era, characterized by continuous contamination among different contexts and genres (Schroeder, 2005). On one hand, many artists conceived of themselves as brands (e.g.,

Andy Warhol) (Schroeder, 2005). On the other hand, many brands have been managed as artworks by progressively including artists in their development. Baumgarth, Neugebauer, & Kristal (2015) notes that by observing street artists, brand managers can get to know more about brands and consumer society. We argue that hybridization occurs when artists have an active role in a brand's development, management, and positioning. An example of brand positioning obtained through artification is the Prada Marfa installation, created by artists Michael Elmgreen and Ingar Dragset and placed in the Texas desert. The artwork, which represents a fake Prada boutique and displays the brand's Spring/Summer 2005 collection, has become a Texas landmark, appearing on TV shows such as The Simpsons and Gossip Girl in addition to Beyoncé's Instagram feed (Zara, 2019). According to Kapferer (2017), artified brands can acquire contemporary looks while being faithful to their heritage and create entry barriers to competitor brands.

- *Art-based advertising*: The reference to artworks in advertising has been subject of a number of studies (e.g., Hetsroni & Tukachinsky, 2005). Research has shown that ads incorporating works of art can enhance the advertised products' perceived luxuriousness (Peluso et al., 2017). One of the first artists to be involved in advertising was Touluse Lautrec, with his iconic representations of the Moulin Rouge (Baumgarth, 2018). Dior also employs artists in the development of ads, which resemble art creations so much that they "are to be treated as its bags or dresses" (Kapferer, 2012, p. 458). More recently, Stella McCarthy collaborated with artist Ed Ruscha, who developed the winter campaign #Stellacares, which focuses on the fashion designer's cruelty-free production ethics and shows payoffs such as "Meat Free" and "Veg Out" (Moncayo, 2019).

Conclusion and Introduction to the Chapters

This chapter dealt with the notion of artification (i.e., the transformation of nonart into art and its conceptualization as a process) in the context of luxury fashion companies and brands in order to identify strategies put in place by luxury firms to *artify* their products, namely, synergies, contaminations, and hybridizations. The structure of this book exemplifies such a classification by identifying three sections: Art & Fashion Synergies, Contaminations, and Hybridizations. Sergio Rossi (Chapter 2) represents a fashion business that collaborates with art (i.e., an instance of art and fashion synergies). The case shows how involving artists at the workplace can affect how management and employees perceive and relate to their company and its product and production process, as well as to the local context in which the company is embedded. Chapters 3 and 4 exemplify cases of contaminations in the context of fashion companies (Gucci and Trussardi). In particular, the case of Trussardi displays the mutual positive externalities accrued by two separate organizations: the Nicola Trussardi Foundation, an institution aimed at the promotion of contemporary art, and the Trussardi Fashion Maison. Gucci is an example of a successful Italian company that, despite the fashion industry's complexity, has managed to redefine luxury by bringing art into the world of fashion. Finally, Balenciaga and Dior (Chapters 5 and 6) are instances of a full hybridization process according to which there is no distinction between fashion and art (Jelinek, 2018), as contemporary artists are directly involved in the product creation projects. Characterized by sculptural quality, deft manipulation of textiles, and dramatic use of color and texture, Balenciaga's creations are directly inspired by artworks: Balenciaga is a brand that carries the name of the designer known as "The Master of Haute Couture," one of the most revered and influential fashion designers of the twentieth century. The case of Christian Dior depicts the hybridization process in the case of *Maison Dior* through three kinds of mechanisms: the celebration of the creator as an artist, the heritization process that drives consumers to consider Christian Dior as part of the French heritage, and a piece of French fashion history, the spectacularization of the Maison that maintains the brand's contemporary vision based on creative director's work. All these cases have been selected, as they are exemplary representations of how artification processes translate into business strategies and collaboration that might stand out as sources of companies' competitive advantage.

References

Alexander, V. (1996). From philanthropy to funding: The effects of corporate and public support on American art museums. *Poetics, 24*(2), 87–129.

Ardenne, P. (1995). The art market in the 1980s. *International Journal of Political Economy, 25*(2), 100–128.

Atwood, T. (2014). *H&M's Jeff Koons collaboration is making all our artsy fashion dreams come true.* Retrieved January 22, 2019, from https://www.bustle.com/articles/27896-hms-jeff-koons-collaboration-is-making-all-our-artsy-fashion-dreams-come-true.

Bain & Company. (2018). *Luxury goods worldwide market study.* Retrieved January 22, 2019, from https://www.bain.com/contentassets/8df501b9f8d6442eba00040246c6b4f9/bain_digest__luxury_goods_worldwide_market_study_fall_winter_2018.pdf.

Banes, S. (1994). *Writing dancing in the age of postmodernism.* Hanover: Wesleyan University Press.

Banister, E., & Hogg, M. (2004). Negative symbolic consumption and consumers' drive for self-esteem. *European Journal of Marketing, 38*(7), 850–868.

Bargenda, A. (2019). Aesthetic CSR Communication: A global perspective on organizational art collections. In A. Bartoli, J. L. Guerrero, & P. Hermel (Eds.), *Responsible organizations in the global context* (pp. 117–132). Cham: Palgrave Macmillan.

Batat, W. (2019). Transforming luxury brand experiences through artification: A marketing and consumer research perspective. *Marche et Organisations, 2,* 135–151.

Baumgarth, C. (2018). Brand management and the world of the arts: Collaboration, co-operation, co-creation, and inspiration. *Journal of Product & Brand Management, 27*(3), 237–248.

Baumgarth, C., Lohrisch, N., & Kastner, O. L. (2014). Arts meet luxury brands. In B. Berghaus, G. Müller-Stewens, & S. Reinecke (Eds.), *The management of luxury: A practioner's handbook* (pp. 157–171). London: Kogan Page Limited.

Baumgarth, C., Neugebauer, F., & Kristal, S. (2015). Brand play and brand attack by artists. In *Proceedings of the AIMAC Conference.* Retrieved from http://cbaumgarth.net/wp-content/uploads/2017/07/Brand-play-and-brand-attack_aimac2017.pdf. Accessed 20 April, 2020.

Benjamin, W. (2008). *The work of art in the age of its technological reproducibility, and other writings on media.* Harvard University Press.
Beverland, M. B. (2005). Crafting brand authenticity: The case of luxury wines. *Journal of Management Studies, 42*(5), 1003–1029.
Carrillat, F. A., D'astous, A., & Colbert, F. (2008). The effectiveness of art venue sponsorship: An attribution perspective. *Journal of Sponsorship, 1*(3), 274–285.
Carù, A., Ostillio, M. C., & Leone, G. (2017). Corporate museums to enhance brand authenticity in luxury goods companies: The case of Salvatore Ferragamo. *International Journal of Arts Management, 19*(2), 32–45.
Caves, R. E. (2000). *Creative industries: Contracts between art and commerce.* Cambridge, MA.: Harvard University Press.
Chailan, C. (2018). Art as a means to recreate luxury brands' rarity and value. *Journal of Business Research, 85*(April), 414–423.
Chailan, C., & Valek, I. (2014). Preserving luxury exclusively through art. In B. Berghaus, G. Müller-Stewens, & S. Reinecke (Eds.), *The management of luxury: A practioner's handbook* (pp. 57–171). London: Kogan Page Limited.
Chen, V. (2016). *Why Tod's renovated the Colosseum, and why Bulgari repaired the Spanish steps, while Fendi threw millions into a fountain.* Retrieved February 3, 2020, from https://www.scmp.com/magazines/style/tech-design/article/1995564/italian-heritage-why-tods-renovated-colosseum-and-why.
Chu, W., Jung, B., & Kim, H. (2010). The Influence of Art Infusion Type on Product Evaluation: Functional Product vs. Hedonic Product. *Journal of Consumer Studies, 21*(4), 43–69.
Codignola, F., & Rancati, E. (2016). The blending of luxury fashion brands and contemporary art: A global strategy for value creation. In A. Vecchi & C. Buckley (Eds.), *Handbook of research on global fashion management and merchandising* (pp. 50–76). Hershey: IGI Global.
Comunian, R. (2009). Toward a new conceptual framework for business investments in the arts: Some examples from Italy. *The Journal of Arts Management, Law, and Society, 39*(3), 200–220.
Creux, G. (2012). Nathalie Heinich, Roberta Shapiro (dir.), De l'artification. Enquêtes sur le passage à l'art. *Lectures.*
Crewe, L. (2016). Placing fashion: Art, space, display and the building of luxury fashion markets through retail design. *Progress in Human Geography, 40*(4), 511–529.
DiMaggio, P. (1982). Cultural entrepreneurship in nineteenth-century Boston: The creation of an organizational base for high culture in America. *Media, Culture and Society, 4*(1), 33–50.

DiMaggio, P. (1988). Interest and agency in institutional theory. In L. G. Zucker (Ed.), *Research on institutional patterns: Environment and culture* (pp. 3–21). Cambridge: Ballinger Publishing Co.

Dion, D., & Arnould, E. (2011). Retail luxury strategy: Assembling charisma through art and magic. *Journal of Retailing, 87*(4), 502–520.

Dissanayake, E. (2011). Doing without the ideology of art. *New Literary History, 42*(1), 71–79. Project MUSE. https://doi.org/10.1353/nlh.2011.0010.

Dubois, B., Laurent, G., & Czellar, S. (2001). *Consumer rapport to luxury: Analyzing complex and ambivalent attitudes* (HEC Research Papers Series No. 736). Jouy-en-Josas, France: HEC Paris.

Erjavec, A. (2012). Artification and the aesthetic regime of art. *Contemporary Aesthetics, 4,* 8–18.

Estes, Z., Brotto, L., & Busacca, B. (2018). The value of art in marketing: An emotion-based model of how artworks in ads improve product evaluations. *Journal of Business Research, 85*(April), 396–405.

Firat, A. F., & Venkatesh, A. (1995). Liberatory postmodernism and the reenchantment of consumption. *Journal of Consumer Research, 22*(3), 239–267.

Finkel, R. (2010). Re-imaging arts festivals through a corporate lens: A case study of business sponsorship at the Henley Festival. *Managing Leisure, 15*(4), 237–250.

Geczy, A., & Karaminas, V. (2012). *Fashion and art.* London: Berg.

Godey, B., Lagier, J., & Pederzoli, D. (2009). A measurement scale of "aesthetic style" applied to luxury goods stores. *International Journal of Retail and Distribution Management, 37*(6), 527–537.

Hagtvedt, H., & Patrick, V. M. (2008a). Art infusion: The influence of visual art on the perception and evaluation of consumer products. *Journal of Marketing Research, 45*(3), 379–389.

Hagtvedt, H., & Patrick, V. M. (2008b). Art and the brand: The role of visual art in enhancing brand extendibility. *Journal of Consumer Psychology, 18*(3), 212–222.

Heinich, N., & Shapiro, R. (2012a, May 15). *De l'artification: Une réponse à Gérard Creux.* Retrieved February 6, 2020, from http://journals.openedition.org/lectures/8395.

Heinich, N., & Shapiro, R. (Eds.). (2012b). *De l'artification: Enquêtes sur le passage à l'art* (Vol. 20). Éditions de l'École des Hautes Études en Sciences Sociales.

Hetsroni, A., & Tukachinsky, R. (2005). The use of fine art in advertising: A survey of creatives and content analysis of advertisements. *Journal of Current Issues and Research in Advertising, 27*(1), 93–107.

Holt, D. B. (2002). Why do brands cause trouble? A dialectical theory of consumer culture and branding. *Journal of Consumer Research, 29*(1), 70–90.
Jelinek, J. S. (2018). Art as strategic branding tool for luxury fashion brands. *Journal of Product and Brand Management, 27*(3), 294–307.
Jin, B., & Cedrola, E. (Eds.). (2016). *Palgrave studies in practice: Global fashion brand management.* New York: Palgrave Macmillan.
Jin, B., & Cedrola, E. (Eds.). (2017). *Fashion branding and communication: Core strategies of European luxury brands.* New York: Palgrave Mcmillian.
Joy, A., Wang, J. J., Chan, T.-S., Sherry, J. F., Jr., & Cui, G. (2014). M(art) worlds: Consumer perceptions of how luxury brand stores become art institutions. *Journal of Retailing, 90*(3), 347–364.
Kapferer, J.-N. (2012). Abundant rarity: The key to luxury growth. *Business Horizons, 55*(5), 453–462.
Kapferer, J.-N. (2014). The artification of luxury: From artisans to artists. *Business Horizons, 57*(3), 371–380.
Kapferer, J.-N. (2015). *Kapferer on luxury: How luxury brands can grow yet remain rare.* London: Kogan Page.
Kapferer, J.-N. (2017). *Lusso: Nuove sfide, nuovi sfidanti.* Milano: FrancoAngeli.
Kapferer, J.-N., & Bastien, V. (2009). *The luxury strategy: Break the rules of marketing to build luxury brands.* London: Kogan Page.
Kapferer, J.-N., & Bastien, V. (2012). *The luxury strategy: Break the rules of marketing to build luxury brands.* Kogan page publishers.
Kastner, O. L. (2013). *When luxury meets art: Forms of collaboration between luxury brands and the arts.* Berlin: Springer Science & Business Media.
Kim, S. B. (1998). Is fashion art? *Fashion Theory, 2*(1), 51–71.
Kim, K., Ko, E., & Lee, Y. I. (2012). Art infusion in fashion product: The influence of visual art on product evaluation and purchase intention of consumers. *Journal of Global Fashion Marketing, 3*(4), 180–186.
Kim, P., Chang, H., Vaidyanathan, R., & Stoel, L. (2018). Artist-brand alliances to target new consumers: Can visual artists recruit new consumers to a brand? *Journal of Product & Brand Management, 27*(3), 308–319.
Koronaki, E., Kyrousi, A. G., & Panigyrakis, G. G. (2018). The emotional value of arts-based initiatives: Strengthening the luxury brand–consumer relationship. *Journal of Business Research, 85*(April), 406–413.
Kottasz, R., Bennett, R., Savani, S., & Ali-Choudhury, R. (2008). The role of corporate art in the management of corporate identity. *Corporate Communications: an International Journal, 13*(3), 235–254.

Kubler, A., & Smith, M. O. (2013). *Art/fashion in the 21st century*. London: Thames and Hudson Ltd.
LeClair, M., & Doornbosch, K. (1995). Corporate acquisitions of fine art: Measuring the underlying motivation. *Managerial Finance, 21*(6), 1–15.
Lee, J., & Han, Y. (2010). Effect of art infusion on consumer evaluation: Focusing on product types. *Korean Journal of Consumer and Advertising Psychology, 11*(4), 792–821.
Lee, J., & Han, Y. (2011). Effects of art infusion on luxury perceptions: Focus on the moderating effects of product and brand concept types. *The Korean Journal of Advertising, 22*(5), 69–97.
Lee, H. C., Chen, W. W., & Wang, C. W. (2015). The role of visual art in enhancing perceived prestige of luxury brands. *Marketing Letters, 26*(4), 593–606.
Lipovetsky, G., & Manlow, V. (2009). The 'artialization' of luxury stores. In J. Brand & J. Teunissen (Eds.), *Fashion and imagination—About clothes and art* (pp. 154–167). Arnhem, The Netherlands: ArtEZ Press.
Martorella, R. (1990). *Corporate art*. New Brunswick: Rutgers University Press.
Massi, M. (2020). *From arts to marketing: The relevance of authenticity in contemporary consumer culture*. London: Palgrave.
Maynard, M. (2012). Clothing: Art clothes or wearable art. In A. Geczy & V. Karaminas (Eds.), *Fashion and art*. London: Berg.
McNicholas, B. (2004). Arts, culture and business: A relationship transformation, a nascent field. *International Journal of Arts Management, 7*(1), 57–69.
Mermiri, T. (2010). Arts sponsorship: The facts, trends, and potential. *Journal of Sponsorship, 3*(3), 307–320.
Meyer, J. W., & Rowan, B. (1977). Institutionalized organizations: Formal structure as myth and ceremony. *American Journal of Sociology, 83*(2), 340–363.
Miller, S. (2007). Fashion as art; is fashion art? *Fashion Theory, 11*(1), 25–40.
Moncayo, M. (2019). *Top 10 most iconic art and fashion collaborations*. Retrieved 6 February, 2020, from https://magazine.artland.com/top-10-iconic-art-fashion-collaborations/.
Montblanc. (2020). *Montblanc de la Culture*. Retrieved 22 January, 2020, from https://www.montblanc.com/en-shop/discover/arts-and-culture/montblanc-de-la-culture.html?glCountry=US.
Morato, A. R. (2003). The culture society: A new place for the arts in the twenty-first century. *The Journal of Arts Management, Law and Society, 32*(4), 245–256.

Naletelich, K., & Paswan, A. K. (2018). Art infusion in retailing: The effect of art genres. *Journal of Business Research, 85*(April), 514–522.
Nia, A., & Zaichkowsky, L. J. (2000). Do counterfeits devalue the ownership of luxury brands? *Journal of Product & Brand Management, 9*(7), 485–497.
Okonkwo, U. (2009). The luxury brand strategy challenge. *Journal of Brand Management, 16*(5–6), 287–289.
Paolino, C. (2019). *Le corporate collection in Italia: Dalla ricerca alla prassi* [Corporate Collection in Italy: From research to practice]. Bologna: Il Mulino.
Paolino, C., Bissola, R., & Imperatori, B.. (2018). Practices combination and collections' configurations: A complementarity-based approach to corporate collections. In P. Canonico & S. C. G. M. M. M. R. M. L. M. (Eds.), *Organizing in the shadow of power* (pp. 607–630). Rome, Italy: Studi MOA.
Park, C. W., Jaworski, B. J., & MacInnis, D. J. (1986). Strategic brand concept-image management. *Journal of Marketing, 50*(4), 135–145.
Passebois-Ducros, J., Trinquecoste, J. F., & Pichon, F. (2015). Stratégies d'artification dans le domaine du luxe Le cas des vins de prestige. *Décisions Marketing, 80*(October–December), 109–124.
Peluso, A. M., Pino, G., Amatulli, C., & Guido, G. (2017). Luxury advertising and recognizable artworks: New insights on the "art infusion" effect. *European Journal of Marketing, 51*(11/12), 2192–2206.
Phau, I., & Siew Leng, Y. (2008). Attitudes toward domestic and foreign luxury brand apparel. *Journal of Fashion Marketing and Management: An International Journal, 12*(1), 68–89.
Piacentini, M., & Mailer, G. (2004). Symbolic consumption in teenagers' clothing choices. *Journal of Consumer Behaviour, 3*(3), 251–262.
Quester, P. G., & Thompson, B. (2001). Advertising and promotion leverage on arts sponsorship effectiveness. *Journal of Advertising Research, 41*(1), 33–47.
Rodner, V. L., & Kerrigan, F. (2014). The art of branding – lessons from visual artists. *Arts Marketing: an International Journal, 4*(1/2), 101–118.
Rolex (2020). *Perpetuating culture.* Retrieved 22 January, 2020, from https://www.rolex.org/en/arts. Accessed on October 27, 2019.
Schroeder, J. E. (2005). The artist and the brand. *European Journal of Marketing, 39*(11/12), 1291–1305.
Schwaiger, M., Sarstedt, M., & Taylor, C. R. (2010). Art for the sake of the corporation: Audi, BMW group, DaimlerChrysler, Montblanc, Siemens, and Volkswagen help explore the effect of sponsorship on corporate reputations. *Journal of Advertising Research, 50*(1), 77–90.

Shapiro, R. (2004a). The aesthetics of institutionalization: Breakdancing in France. *The Journal of Arts Management, Law, and Society, 33*(4), 316–335.

Shapiro, R. (2004b). Qu'est-ce que l'artification? XVIIth Congress of the International Association of Sociology of French Language, "The Individual Social," Tours.

Shapiro, R. (2012). Du smurf au ballet. L'invention de la danse hip-hop. In N. Heinich, & R. Shapiro (Eds.), *De l'artification. Enquêtes sur le passage à l'art.* Paris: école des hautes études en sciences sociales.

Shapiro, R. (2019). Artification as process. *Cultural Sociology, 13*(3), 265–275.

Shapiro, R., & Heinich, N. (2012). When is artification? *Contemporary Aesthetics, 9*(4), 1–17.

Shusterman, R. (1991). The fine art of rap. *New Literary History, 22*(3), 613–632.

Simon, M. (1995). *Fashion in art: The second empire and Impressionism.* London and Paris: Hazan.

Sjöholm, J., & Pasquinelli, C. (2014). Artist brand building: Towards a spatial perspective. *Arts Marketing: an International Journal, 4*(1/2), 10–24.

Soito, P. (2018). *Why art is the cornerstone of luxury brands.* Retrieved February 6, 2020, from http://artmarketmag.com/why-art-is-the-cornerstone-of-luxury-brands/.

Steele, V. (2012a). Fashion. In A. Geczy & V. Karaminas (Eds.), *Fashion and art.* London: Berg.

Steele, V. (2012b). *Is fashion art?* [video file]. Retrieved February 6, 2020, from https://youtu.be/weB-SQ-XP-c.

Tarrant, S., & Jolles, M. (2012). *Fashion talks: Undressing the power of style.* Albany: State University of New York Press.

Teunissen, J. (2009). Fashion and art. In J. Brand & J. Teunissen (Eds.), *Fashion and imagination—About clothes and art* (pp. 10–25). Arnhem, Netherlands: ArtEZ Press.

Tokatli, N. (2014). Made in Italy? Who cares! Prada's new economic geography. *Geoforum, 54,* 1–9.

Trilling, L. (1972). *Sincerity and authenticity.* Cambridge, MA: Harvard University Press.

Vacca, F. (2014). Knowledge in memory: Corporate and museum archives. *Fashion Practice, 6*(2), 273–288.

Vukadin, A., Lemoine, J. F., & Badot, O. (2016). Opportunities and risks of combining shopping experience and artistic elements in the same store: A contribution to the magical functions of the point of sale. *Journal of Marketing Management, 32*(9–10), 944–964.

Vukadin, A., Wongkitrungrueng, A., & Assarut, N. (2018). When art meets mall: Impact on shopper responses. *Journal of Product & Brand Management, 27*(3), 277–293.
Weissman, P. (1967). The art of fashion. *The Metropolitan Museum of Art Bulletin, 26*(3), 151–152.
Wilson, E. (1987). *Adorned in dreams.* Berkeley: University of California Press.
Worth, M. (2016). *Fundraising: Principles and practice.* Los Angeles: Sage.
Wu, C. (2002). The relationship of ethical decision-making to business ethics and performance in Taiwan. *Journal of Business Ethics, 35*(3), 163–176.
Zara. (2019). Prada in the desert: How a fake luxury boutique became a Texas landmark. *The Guardian.* Retrieved October 27, 2019, from https://www.theguardian.com/us-news/2019/oct/03/prada-marfa-texas-sculpture-boutique.

2

Sergio Rossi and Its Magic Kingdom: Artistic Interventions, Brand Identity Renewal, and Stakeholder Awareness

Chiara Paolino and Ariane Berthoin Antal

Abstract This chapter explores how artification achieved through artistic interventions can enhance brand identity renewal in an organization and, thereby, expand the CSR approach of luxury fashion companies. We conducted an exploratory study on Sergio Rossi, the iconic Italian luxury brand for leather shoes. Sergio Rossi launched a creative process to renew its brand and company identity by reemphasizing the role of the factory, its Magic Kingdom. This case integrates CSR literature with artification by moving beyond positioning art collections as a philanthropic CSR activity. It shows how involving artists at the workplace can affect how management and employees perceive and relate to their company, its product and production process, as well as to the local context

C. Paolino (✉)
Università Cattolica Del Sacro Cuore, Milan, Italy
e-mail: chiara.paolino@unicatt.it

A. Berthoin Antal
WZB Berlin Social Science Center, Berlin, Germany
e-mail: ariane.berthoin.antal@wzb.eu

M. Massi and A. Turrini (eds.), *The Artification of Luxury Fashion Brands*,
Palgrave Studies in Practice: Global Fashion Brand Management,
https://doi.org/10.1007/978-3-030-26121-4_2

in which the company is embedded. This chapter proposes a research agenda to study the dynamics and the outcomes of artistic interventions in different cultural settings and recommends enriching CSR research with notions from artification and aesthetic theory.

Keywords Artistic interventions · Art & brand synergies · Corporate social responsibility · Sergio Rossi

Introduction

Corporate art collections are usually treated by economists as investments and by organizational theorists as a philanthropic dimension of corporate social responsibility (Lewandowska, 2015). While there is some value in both these perspectives, they are too limited because they isolate the arts from the dynamics of organizational behavior. They do not consider how artification processes in an organization may affect how members of the organization perceive the nature of the business and its relation to society. Emerging research on artistic interventions in organizations has documented many ways in which engaging with the arts can influence perceptions, ideas, and behaviors at the individual, group, and organizational level (Berthoin Antal, 2014; Darsø, 2004). Might it, therefore, be possible for the introduction of art into an organization to affect the actual nature of corporate and brand identity, and social responsibility?

Emerging literature is beginning to explore how art can affect the perception of a brand on different levels, including "inspiration, insights, identity and image" (Baumgarth, 2018, p. 237). In the fashion industry, the connection between art and company identity, image and brand has been analyzed in response to urgent calls for empirical research to address how authenticity is perceived in the field (Carroll, 2015; Carù, Ostillio, & Leone, 2017). In the broader arena of luxury goods, studies have examined the relationship between art and company identity and image mainly from the consumers' perspective (e.g., Beverland, 2006). This chapter focuses specifically on how artification through artistic interventions at the workplace can affect the perception and the meaning of brand and company identity and how they could stimulate an awareness of a broader range of stakeholders in corporate social responsibility. To this end, we conducted interviews with artists, management, and employees in an Italian fashion company, Sergio Rossi S.p.A., which embarked on an experiment with contemporary artists. This project implies a new way of conceiving the factory, which the CEO has named "The Magic Kingdom." The insights gained from our interviews suggest that artification occurring through interactions between the artist and the organization's employees, materials, history, and environment can expand the understanding and sharpen the focus of the organization's responsibility and identity in society.

This chapter is organized as follows. First, it provides an overview on the company and explains its suitability for this exploratory study. Secondly, it provides the theoretical framework, drawing together threads from research on corporate social responsibility, artistic interventions, artification, and aesthetics that have not been connected to date. In addition, it explains the data collection and analysis process. Third, it presents and discusses the findings from the interviews with the managers and artists about the intention of the art projects, and then about the experience itself, including views from some employees. Finally, it summarizes the conclusions, suggests future research angles, and provides recommendations for managers interested in bringing art into their organization, especially in the luxury fashion industry.

Company Overview

In order to examine our research questions, we looked for a luxury brand that was engaging with the arts and was willing to allow us to conduct an exploratory study to learn about the perspectives of managers, artists, and employees. We chose Sergio Rossi S.p.A, an Italian company that designs, produces, distributes, and sells leather shoes and leather accessories for women and men. It is known and respected in the shoemaking sector for its artisanship and the iconic models it created.

The case of this company is particularly suitable for this investigation for several reasons. First, the fashion industry is showing increased attention to art in the context of seeking to become more authentic and sustainable (Baumgarth, 2018). Second, the management of Sergio Rossi decided to start the process of identity change by focusing on the manufacturing process and the factory—their Magic Kingdom—rather than driving the change as a brand strategy project. This unusual approach offers the opportunity to study the interaction between art and the corporate setting even beyond consumers' perception, especially in the fashion industry. The presence of art in fashion companies is not new (Masè & Silchenko, 2017); however, the collaboration between art and the fashion industry has been mainly focused on the direct participation of the artist in the business processes. The common types of initiatives include the collaboration of an artist on designing the product, artists' participation to the advertising campaign for the products, the sponsorship of artists' work in cultural institutions, and the creation of a special design for windows and stores dedicated to an artist's works (Masè & Cedrola, 2017).

By contrast, the case of Sergio Rossi illustrates how it can be effective to organize a collaboration that is meant to explore and clarify the company's identity and processes by working on the aesthetics of the workplace and the employees, rather than a direct intervention on the product. This exploratory study considers the experiences generated by artistic intervention residencies with three contemporary Italian artists: Davide Allieri, Ettore Favini, and Vedovamazzei.

Company History

In 1951 Sergio Rossi, the son of an artisan shoemaker, founded the company, to which he gave his own name. The company expanded during the 1980s and the 1990s. In these years, the presence of the Rossi family was very strong in the company, and the founder was a point of reference for employees and clients. In 1999, the Gucci group acquired the Sergio Rossi brand, in 2005 the Kering Group, the owner of Gucci, acquired the whole company; then in 2016, Investindustrial, an Italian investment fund, took over Sergio Rossi. At the time of our study in 2019, Sergio Rossi had 294 employees and distributed in 14 countries around the world through 45 sales points and 10 franchises. The heart of the company, where 219 of the 294 employees work, is in San Mauro Pascolo in Rimini. The commercial offices are in Milan.

What makes the Sergio Rossi case particularly interesting for our purpose is the process of identity renewal that was initiated after new management arrived in 2016. This renewal process started out by emphasizing the role that the factory has had in the company for many years and that it will play in the future. When Riccardo Sciutto took over as CEO he decided to inaugurate a new "Italian" era, in which the production process is conceived as the core of the company identity, the place where the shoes are designed, prototyped, and created. The factory is considered to be the place where the history and the tradition of the company materially encounter the opportunities that new markets and technology may open up. Since 2016, the management of Sergio Rossi has worked to elaborate and spread the idea of its new identity as an Italian luxury shoe production company, where the actual making process is at the heart of the way the company wants to propose itself to its own employees and external stakeholders. Riccardo Sciutto's motto is "*Think heritage, Play digital*," expressing the intention to combine tradition and modernity.

Artification Strategy

In this section we show how Sergio Rossi represents an exemplary instance of artification based on synergies between the brand and the art world (see Chapter 1). In particular, we delve into the concept of artistic interventions building on the CSR literature and aesthetic theory. We illustrate the artification process of the Sergio Rossi brand by presenting the results of an exploratory study conducted with artists, management, and employees in the company.

Corporate Social Responsibility, Brand Identity, and the Arts

The literature on corporate social responsibility has traditionally distinguished between economic, legal, ethical, and philanthropic responsibilities (Carroll, 1979). A drawback inherent in the traditional differentiation between the four aspects of CSR is that they have tended to be treated separately and associated with different stakeholders. Philanthropy has been considered as externally focused on stakeholders in society, whereas the responsibility to employees as internal stakeholders is usually seen as part of legal and ethical responsibilities.

The concept and practice of CSR has evolved over the years (Carroll, 1999; Garriga & Melé, 2004) and different terms have been introduced to address the relationship between the types of responsibilities and the stakeholders involved. For example, Wood (1991) introduced a framework for addressing the outcome of CSR as corporate social performance; the notion of corporate citizenship attempted to integrate corporate social responsibility and performance with stakeholder theory (Waddock, 2004); and the concept of global responsibility offered an approach to address the interconnectedness of the themes and stakeholders at the local, national, and international levels (Berthoin Antal & Sobczak, 2004). However, CSR scholars have paid little attention to how engaging with the arts can relate to different aspects of CSR and connect different internal and external stakeholders.

Corporate activities related to the arts have generally been associated with philanthropic support for culture in society. The traditional narrow focus on arts only as a philanthropic activity overlooks the fact that companies have also engaged with the arts in other ways, outside the traditional realm of CSR. Probably the oldest type of business relationship with the arts is the corporate art collection. Many such collections may still just be about "personal aggrandizement, organizational prestige, and long-term investment and the decoration of the work environment" (Barry & Meisiek, 2010, p. 1511).

However, some collectors are coming to view their art collections as a possible resource for learning to see and think differently in the organization. For example, the American magnate Albert C. Barnes, who wanted to edify his employees through art in the first quarter of the twentieth century. More recently, EA Generali in Austria and Novo Nordisk in Denmark intended for their collections to provoke and irritate, thereby generating "creative unrest" and signaling to employees that unusual ideas and projects are welcome in the organization (Barry & Meisiek, 2010, p. 1512). It is this spirit that has underpinned many recent experiments with artistic interventions in organizations, bringing people, practices, and products from the world of the arts into organizations for hours, days, months, and even years (Berthoin Antal, 2014).

Recently, scholars have argued that corporate art collections, and, more widely, of artistic interventions at the workplace, could be conceived of as a form of CSR investment for the potential of art to stimulate companies—especially those in the luxury field—to go beyond considering customers as the preferred stakeholders for discussing their brand perception. Artification through artistic interventions might offer a fresh way for companies to interact with a variety of stakeholders, ranging from employees and customers, to competitors and the local community, and to engage with them in discussing and renewing its own identity (Paolino, 2019a). For instance, the exhibition "*Sustainable Thinking*," organized in 2019 by the Salvatore Ferragamo Museum to discuss the topic of sustainability, is a way for this company to connect with a wider group of stakeholders to propose and discuss its identity. The exhibition involved the local community by displaying the artworks not only in the Salvatore Ferragamo Museum venue, but also in public museums and exhibition centers in Florence.

Moreover, educational activities along with conferences and talks were organized in the city and in schools. The exhibition was also a way to establish a new relationship with the employees, since artists were invited to experiment with the company materials and production processes and diverse functions were called to collaborate in an integrated manner to create sustainable products to be exhibited. Finally, the exhibition offered a way to establish a new relationship with suppliers and competitors, showing the company's desire to be sustainable and be recognized as such (Paolino, 2019b). This example illustrates the potential of artification—in terms of corporate engagement with the arts—to enlarge the perspective of a company, when considering the wider set of stakeholders with whom it aims to discuss its own identity.

Research on artistic interventions in organizations has not yet explicitly addressed CSR, but the findings open avenues for investigating possible connections. Most of the studies on artistic interventions have focused on the processes and outcomes of projects in which artists engaged directly with employees in organizations. The entrance of artists into non-arts-based organizations has been found to open an "interspace" in which the usual norms are temporarily suspended, thereby enabling the expression and exploration of new ideas and behaviors, which individuals and groups can choose to take forward afterwards (Berthoin Antal & Strauß, 2016). Engaging with artists in interventions usually stimulates questions and reflections about individual and organizational identity and the meaning of work. The fact that artists are perceived to come from a world other than that of managers and business consultants—a world in which emotions of all kinds matter, and a world in which authenticity is valued—appears to be crucial for opening the hearts and minds of employees at all levels of the organization.

Among the potentially relevant effects for CSR that participants in artistic interventions often find are that the experience led them to challenge engrained assumptions, expand their horizons, and clarify their individual and collective sense of purpose (Berthoin Antal & Strauß, 2016). Furthermore, respondents often report that working with artists led to the creation of new relationships with stakeholders outside the organization. For example, in the case of an artistic intervention in an Italian company producing extractor fans, an artist spent almost a year in the company, producing extensive "intermediate" works before arriving at the final artwork (Paolino, Smarrelli, & Carè, 2018).

Throughout this long process, the artist engaged with a variety of stakeholders. She wanted to work on a new idea of aspirators that could purify the air. These aspirators were not meant to exist or to work in any way, they were to remain research objects within the company. To develop her project, the artist first involved the operators in the factory, working with them, using their materials and drawings, and reinterpreting them. In addition, she involved students in order to understand how to select among the "prototypes" that she created during the time spent in the company. Her final work, together with a book/diary she wrote during this project, was displayed in a public museum with an exhibition, to which the employees were also invited (Paolino et al., 2018). Other studies also offer qualitative evidence that the presence of the artist at the workplace can create a new relationship with stakeholders both inside and outside the company (for a review of such research see Berthoin Antal & Strauß, 2016).

Some studies have also examined the effects of artworks in organizations. They can stimulate individual as well as collective responses. An employee in Germany expressed the value of art in the company enthusiastically: "It brings a fresh breath of air into the daily work and opens new perspectives. It is good for the soul to engage with art!" (Berthoin Antal & Nussbaum Bitran, 2019, p. 67). In a similar vein, employees in a pharmaceutical company in Italy noted that the emotions they felt and the way they had interacted during the artistic interventions were transferable to their job:

> Following this experience, I found myself more able to listen to everyone, especially those who needed help to do their job. I discovered that I was more open to dialoguing and to listening. I thought: 'it felt so natural when the artist was here, and if it comes so naturally during the artistic experience, why I should not push myself to be like that even in my daily job?' (Paolino et al., 2018, p. 83)

Of course not all responses are so enthusiastic, and although most of the research on the effects of artistic interventions documents positive responses, it would be naïve to automatically consider them socially responsible. Scholars also warn of the risk of the unethical use of artistic interventions, for example, to manipulate employees (Berthoin Antal, Debucquet, & Frémeaux, 2017). Nevertheless, aesthetic theory indicates that it would be shortsighted to consider less enthusiastic kinds of responses as problematic. As Strati (2000) explained, there are multiple aesthetic categories beyond beauty, such as: grotesque, the comic, the sublime, the ugly, and the sacred. Thus, artworks can evoke different, equally interesting, emotional responses, including anger and disgust.

Unlike managers and consultants, who tend to consider such responses problematic, artists see them as a source of energy with which to engage.

A further finding of research on artworks in organizations is that they can extend the effects of an artistic intervention residency. Follow-up research in a French company in Paris showed that the presence of the artworks—created during the residencies—continued to generate conversations about organizational values both among employees and with external stakeholders several years after the completion of the project (Bessière, 2013).

By contrast, sometimes the impact of the presence of art in organizations becomes particularly evident when the art leaves. For example, when a corporate art collection was dismantled after a foreign company acquired the organization, sales managers expressed their concerns to the curator because they had found the presence of the artworks a generative point of departure for conversations with customers and suppliers (personal communication).

If one of the processes that artistic interventions can trigger is a reflection on identity, it is useful to draw on literature about the relationship between identity and authenticity, particularly in the luxury fashion industry, in which this concept is playing an increasingly important role.

> Authenticity carries moral meaning about the values and choices embedded in an object. A person is said to be authentic, for example, if she is sincere, assumes responsibility for her actions, and makes explicit value-based choices concerning those actions rather than accepting socially imposed values and actions. In parallel, an organization is authentic to the extent that it embodies the chosen values of its founders, owners, or members rather than simply following convention by, say, pursuing profits. (Carroll, 2015, p. 8)

Art is considered as the opposite of something useful or instrumental to pursue a goal. Artistic interventions can help to infuse authenticity in the perception of a company or a brand identity because the artist brings in fresh perspectives that do not belong to the dominant corporate logics of profit and instrumentality (Berthoin Antal, 2016a). Under this perspective, artification can help luxury fashion brands to win back the authenticity that they lost due to the logics of volumes and market expansion (Kapferer, 2012).

In addition, some artists are intrigued by the opportunity to work on company history and origins, since this kind of reflection is important to share a common ground for starting a discussion with the employees. Finally, artistic interventions can stimulate work on identity and authenticity through critical reflexivity and dialogue, which are fundamental for grappling generatively with defensive attitudes that prohibit change and adaptation (Brown & Starkey, 2000). The freedom with which the artist enters the organization can foster reflexivity and learning among the employees, while helping them to create a new meaning associated with collective identity in the organization.

In addition, this judgment of authenticity through art can help a company and its brand to expand the boundaries of its own identity to include the perceptions of diverse external stakeholders. According to Balmer (2008), it is important to discuss the concept of identity from the perspective of multiple stakeholders, rather than limiting it to the company's employees or customers. He notes that addressing identity from the standpoint of stakeholders relates to how individuals and groups define themselves by their relationships with an organizational culture. According to this line of thinking, stakeholders' identification is easier if the company and the brand identities show features that are salient to the stakeholders themselves. Artification through artistic interventions has this peculiarity of being able to stimulate reflection on a company's history and values, while at the same time connecting the brand with external audiences, thanks to the public and universal valence of art. Thus, art and brand synergies developed through artistic interventions have the potential to speak in a sincere way to a wide audience inside and outside the organization.

In the following sections, after outlining our research method, we analyze the Sergio Rossi case in order to understand how artistic interventions can support the process of identity change that the company started with the "Magic Kingdom" project.

Research Method

Data collection for this exploratory study took the form of interviews with the key actors in the arts project, and a written survey of some employees on the shop floor. The first author also visited the company with the director of the factory and the curator of the artistic project. The interviews with the CEO, the curator of the artistic intervention residency project, and the three artists were recorded and transcribed. The interviews lasted between 40 and 120 minutes and they revolved around the exploration of: the company identity; the artistic interventions; how respondents relate company identity and the interventions; whether and how there was a reflection on the broader social role of the company through the artistic intervention. It was not possible to interview employees during work time, however the company distributed our questions and two employees responded in writing. The interviews and written materials were in Italian, so the first author (who had conducted the interviews) translated the relevant passages for the second author, after both had agreed on analytical categories drawn from the literature review. We discussed the interpretation iteratively in connection with the literature (Creswell, 1994). In addition, we drew on a variety of documents related to the project: company documents on Sergio Rossi history, on the artistic and archive projects; previous interviews with the artists, the curators and the CEO; books and essays about the artists participating to the project.

Introducing the Magic Kingdom of Sergio Rossi

The process of identity renewal at Sergio Rossi started with a reorganization of the factory and a process of internalization of all the phases for the shoe production. The idea was to give back to artisans the full view of the product and full ownership of its production. The CEO of Sergio Rossi, Riccardo Sciutto, explained in the interview:

(...) The first thing I wanted to do strategically for the business and for the identity of the company was to invest in making the production process and the shop floor crucial again for the success and the identification of the workers and the employees. We were one of the few companies in Italy with the ability to produce more than 1000 shoes a day in terms of production capacity. And we were not doing it, because people and top managers had lost pride in producing along the years and they did not recognize themselves in a production company, while I believed that the manufacturing process was so relevant to have distinctiveness and to honor our true capacity as a company.

(...) I was aware that this process required steps, some technical ones, such as merging the manufacturing company and the legal one, internalizing part of the cutting process that used to be outsourced, and re-establishing a complete new way of managing the factory. But it also required re-introducing emotions and sensitivity somehow within the company and especially at the shop floor, or better, starting from it.

To support the reorganization of the factory, the management wanted to introduce contemporary art and a new archive of the company's products. The combination of these two approaches was significant: management believed that art could bring back emotions to the workplace during the process of renewal, and together with the archival work it could infuse a sense of authenticity by connecting it back to the company roots and tradition. In the interview the CEO explained,

(...) I also started other two processes, the creation of the archive for the company and this first project with contemporary living artists. The archive for me was essential, since there could not be a manufacturing company without the history of the product, the archive had been completely canceled under the past administrations, we had to reacquire first 200 models and then the other 6000, and then all the documents, tools, pictures, articles. Then we digitalized everything and we created three spaces so that everyone in the company could experience this history.

At the same time, I decided I would like to introduce contemporary art in the company (...) I have always rejected the proposal of buying an artwork for the company, since I do not think that something that is still, already done, ready, was going to be ok for us, for the moment we were living, for the emotional experience we were looking for. I wanted to give to Sergio Rossi's people the opportunity to see living art also as way to interpret the archive.

When he was appointed CEO and started the change process, Riccardo Sciutto adopted the metaphor of the *Magic Kingdom* to describe its factory as the place where something extraordinary occurs, which is the shoe production process. The Magic Kingdom brings to mind the idea of a realm where fantastic events might happen. This metaphor represents the spirit of change that the company is going through, identifying the kingdom of wonder with the shop floor and the Italian factory, rather than with other organizational spaces around the world or units within the company.

The Magic Kingdom project started with the artistic intervention residency program that the company launched in 2018 with three contemporary Italian artists, Davide Allieri, Ettore Favini, and Vedovamazzei, representing three different generations, and three different styles and poetics in the Italian artistic context. The company intends to continue with other artists in the future so that the presence of artists and their works will become a constant feature of Sergio Rossi. The company recruited a curator, Rossella Farinotti, to coordinate the project for the next years; the main sponsor and manager of the initiative is the company's CEO, who is supported by the external relations unit. The first step for the artists was to understand the history of the company and to go to the shop floor and try out the production process themselves. The artists were then requested to realize an artwork within the company space; the only instruction they received was to give form to what the history of the company inspired them to do. The main features of the three artistic interventions are described below to illustrate how they interacted with the company setting.

Davide Allieri and Billdor

Davide Allieri, the youngest artist among the three, realized Billdor (see Fig. 2.1). Davide Allieri's work focuses on the concept of display and the contrast between emptiness and fullness of meaning in current society and in communication. Billdor is an empty billboard, three-meter-high,

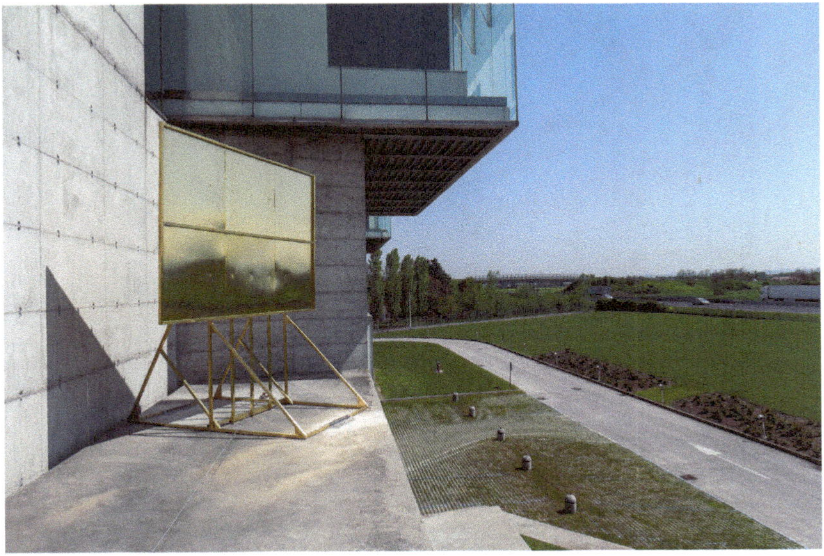

Fig. 2.1 Billdor by Davide Allieri (Reprinted with permission of Sergio Rossi)

completely handmade, and assembled directly at the Sergio Rossi plant. It is located outside the company so the employees see it when they arrive at work every day, and it is very visible from the nearby highway. The idea of realizing a golden Billdor and to locate it outside the company, in a position that metaphorically breaks the landscape, grew out of the artist's desire to express the willingness of the company to go outward, by being visible and by offering itself to the local territory. The emptiness of the billboard also refers to the idea that company history can speak by itself to communicate its own values and tradition externally, without the intervention of the artist creating additional content.

Ettore Favini and Vela al Terzo

Ettore Favini, the artist belonging to the intermediate generation, realized two artworks, entitled *Vela al terzo* (see Fig. 2.2), which is the name of a traditional sail of the Rimini area (Northern Italy) where Sergio Rossi is located. Ettore Favini has already worked with the idea of the sail and

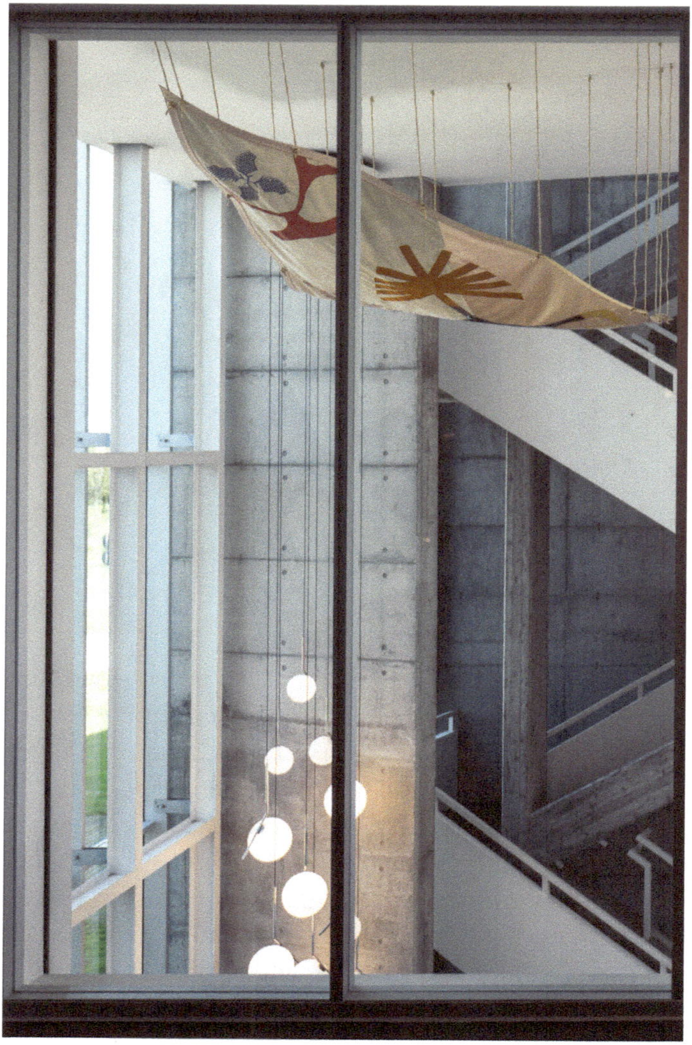

Fig. 2.2 Vela al Terzo by Ettore Favini (Reprinted with permission of Sergio Rossi)

with the idea of a shared production of the sail in his past works. However, his first attempt to produce his artwork in Sergio Rossi did not focus on the idea of the sail, but on the shoes. While walking around the company, his attention was caught by the wooden models of the shoes, which, as the employees proudly explained to him, were manually carved from wood. He was struck by how much the models looked like small sculptures. However, he could not figure out how to use these models in his artwork. One day, hanging out at Rimini's harbor, he noticed the peculiar local sails, *vele al terzo*, and he learned that they used to display symbols of Rimini's families. Thus, the artist decided to work on the project of a sail for the company, but, according to his poetics, he did not think he had the right to decorate the sail himself. His goal was to give a representation of company values and history. He interviewed thirty operators, asking them which was their favorite model of shoes in the entire historical collection, and why they liked that particular one more than other models. From his analysis of the interviews, he found ten models of shoes and very diverse experiences from the operators. Then the artist investigated the original color of the favorite models and he requested full access to the leather archive so that he could find the ideal leather to connect his artwork with the shoes. Thus, by integrating all this information, the artist managed to collect models and materials that represented the operators' most vivid memories of past shoes. His intention was to use these models and material to decorate the sail. Finally, respecting his idea of giving up his authorship to let the communities talk, the artist did not sew the sail himself: he let the operators of Sergio Rossi work on it to make the sail completely theirs. The original sail now hangs in the company's main entry hall. The project was so powerful that the artist decided to make a second piece specifically dedicated to hang in the entrance of the factory. Thus, now it is possible to see two sails in Sergio Rossi, one at the main entrance and the second at the entrance of the factory.

Vedovamazzei and Signature

Vedovamazzei, a duo of Italian artists belonging to the oldest generation of artists in this project, realized *Signature* (see Fig. 2.3), representing the phone number of the company written with the handwriting of the CEO, Riccardo Sciutto. The duo has been working with the idea of identity for a long time and they have been investigating how the current use of technology made phone numbers almost a perfect substitute of people's names. In addition, they have been experimenting with art as a way of playing with the concept of identity in a world where history, roots, traditions are very easily lost. The intention of *Signature* is to reflect Sergio Rossi's identity through its phone number, written by the man who is currently managing the company, who started the art project, but who one day will not be running the company anymore (while the artwork could be still there). This idea of identity, disguise, and irony is also present in the color of *Signature*, which is red when it is turned on, but completely transparent when switched off. Moreover, although

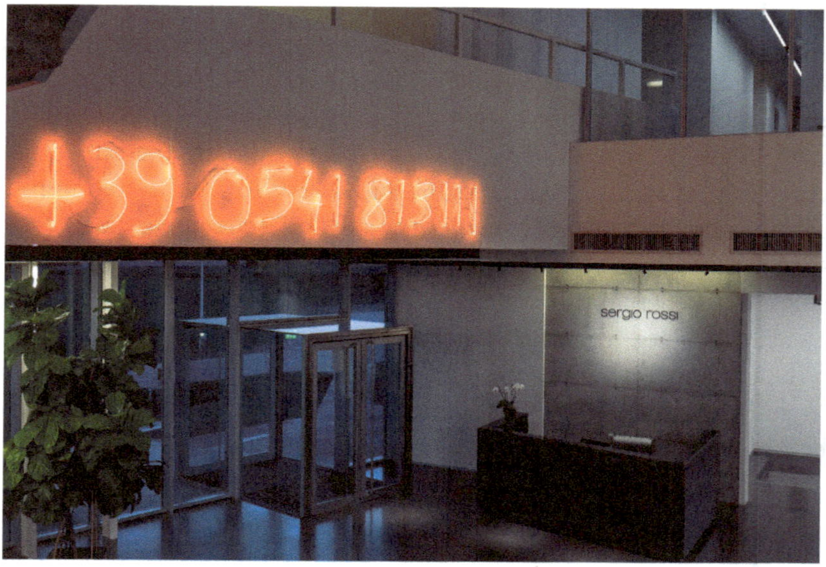

Fig. 2.3 Signature by Vedovamazzei (Reprinted with permission of Sergio Rossi)

Signature looks like an industrial piece, a unique artisan who is an expert in producing glass neon manually crafted the neon.

Archive Project Living Heritage

In parallel with the collaboration with living artists, the CEO started a project dedicated to rebuild the product archive of the company, which he called Living Heritage. The previous management had completely neglected to collect the shoe models they had worked with. The CEO believed that the product archive was an essential step for the new identity of the company. It was the basis for the idea of reinterpreting its history to project the company into the future and building on the centrality of the manufacturing process. The company started by buying back the first 200 models and then the other 6000, as well as all the documents, tools, pictures, and articles about the company, to the founder, and the shoes. The archive is digitalized and there are three spaces dedicated to it, accessible to everyone in the company who is interested in this experience.

The point of view of the curator is also helpful for understanding how artistic interventions can offer different relational experiences for top management and operators, especially for a company that starts this kind of project for the first time. According to Rosella Farinotti, the curator needs to play various roles in this process. One is to find artists who are able to understand the company identity and who can engage in the main processes of the company in ways that do not violate the organizational context with their interventions, nevertheless stimulate emotions and reflections. Another role of the curator is to work with the top management to involve it in the process as well, by making managers aware of the historical and organizational meaning of the artistic interventions. This double approach that the curator described in the process illustrates how much art at the workplace can stimulate a wider and more detailed consideration of stakeholders, in this case, a more fine-grained perception of the employees:

> I wanted to propose something that was right for the historical moment of the company. I started working on the project after having visited the

> company and talked deeply with the CEO, to understand the context. It took me two months to put together the proposal (...) I wanted to propose Italian artists with different poetics, of different age, but also artists with the idea that their work could provide me with references to interpret also the fashion world. Art that, even though so different from the fashion production, could speak to these people also on a more intuitive level; the company deserved not be violated by too detached projects and the projects deserved a key to be understood.
>
> [For the top management] I had and I wanted to explain the origins of the poetics of the artists, why they arrived to that artwork or to that concept, what was their background. I had to explain how Vedovamazzei along the years arrived to conceive this idea of the phone number, of the signature, of the personal identity and of the neon, illustrating the other neons they produced, for which museum, which subjects, how they did arrive there, considering the other medium and subjects they used.

Having illustrated the main features of Sergio Rossi's Magic Kingdom project, in the next section we present our findings on how art has started to contribute to this process of identity regeneration and helped the people in the company to become more aware of and feel more responsible toward Sergio Rossi's stakeholders.

Engaging with the Artists and the Art: Research Findings

In analyzing the case and showing how artification through artistic interventions can contribute to a process of identity renewal, we start with the employees' perspectives, and then look outward at implications for the local territory, for other companies in the fashion industry, and the art system as well.

The Employees: Feeling Proud and Reconnected with the Production Process

The three artistic interventions were meant to refocus the perception of the company identity on the shop floor and to renew the pride in being a made-in-Italy luxury brand producing for the international market. Art was chosen because the CEO believed in the power of art to recreate an emotional link between the employees and the company's new direction. One of the employees expressed his experience in the following words:

> The three artists immediately caught my attention, we were very curious to watch them while they were working, to check whether they were artisans as well and what they were about to do with our shoes (…) Now our workplace has changed a lot, the three artworks have important physical dimensions and now they are part of our daily activities, we see them every day. They are telling a new story about the company, the story of our present, which at the same time goes back to the last 60 years and more.

Another employee also highlighted appreciating the connection between the artists' work and his own:

> I was surprised to see that behind each artwork there was a lot of work, of precision. Behind the artwork, there was a person who worked on it with great effort. To see the relationship between the artist and his work was very interesting and it was exciting to manage to talk and to know the artists while they were in actions in our company spaces.

The CEO expressed his own emotional response to the artists and his feeling that it was palpable in the company:

> I wanted to do something for the company and for the people to reestablish the emotions of being proud to produce shoes. Somehow, contemporary art is close to what we do in our company, because not only do we make objects that are the results of a creative, 'higher', thinking, but also because it takes time to master a shoe, as it takes time to master an artistic process or idea, as much conceptual as it can be. So in having

> living artists within our walls, I found something that could be in continuity with the past, but at the same time to introduce emotions and ways of doing, which are disruptive and unique. It happened like that, I felt an immediate understanding with the artists and this was so important for me to know that I was doing something in the right direction. This spontaneous empathy was also present when the artist worked in the company.

The artists also reflected on the emotional aspect of the process with the employees. This is especially true of Favini, who spent time in the company interviewing operators and investigating the way they related to past products and materials in the current times. His insights into the shift from resistance to feeling "blessed" are significant:

> At the very beginning, I encountered resistance, since I wanted to get in their laboratories and archives, I wanted to work with their materials and I was asking them questions. But later the operators were very happy to talk, to participate to my investigation, to give me the gift of their materials and knowledge (…) I collected also anecdotes from them, for instance from the person who has to try the models and who joked about the fact that they had always the wrong shoes with respect to the seasons. I also got emails from some of them telling me that they felt like blessed every time they passed beneath the sail.

Connecting with the Local Community

Artistic interventions can stimulate employees and management to take a fresh look at the local community and the reciprocity that could exist between the company and the local territory itself. The power of artistic intervention to foster this attention of the company toward the local community in the desire to contribute to it has been already documented in extant literature (Berthoin Antal & Nussbaum-Bitran, 2015). In the case of Sergio Rossi, the company, the artists, and the employees discovered progressively how much these artistic interventions helped the company to look outward, to be more aware of its physical and conceptual positioning within the community of San Mauro Pascoli. The work by Davide Allieri, for instance, is located outside the company. It provides to the external community a sign that the company is there and that it is important for that area. Working with living artist triggered the company to reinforce the idea of participating in a circular system, animated by the feeling of reciprocity. This idea of reciprocity is different from other philanthropic activities the company was already doing, as the CEO explained:

> (…) We have a foundation, but it supports local museums and cultural projects, working with living artists could also serve this idea of circularity between the inner and the external community of the company in a different way.

The research that Ettore Favini undertook to prepare his artwork also implies this connection of the company with the local community. His walk along the Rimini harbor inspired him to do something that was specific to this geographical area. He then searched for the heraldic insignia of the Rossi family in Rimini to make the connection between the sails' decoration, company history and the history of Rimini and San Mauro even more intertwined.

Relating to Other Companies

The experience with these artistic intervention residencies encouraged the CEO to open the company more to other organizations within the same industry and from other companies in the same local area. This extension occurred because the artistic interventions promoted somehow such a feeling of pride and idiosyncrasy of the history of the company and its production process that the company could reveal even more of itself. Working at the same time on the structure of the factory, its processes, the archive, and the artistic interventions has made the Sergio Rossi identity project so unique that the company felt it could be imitated, thereby liberating the company from the fear of hosting visitors. The CEO explained how his feelings changed:

> Since I started this project, I try also to be as open as I can to external visitors. A company from a completely different sector asked whether we could host a team-building activity here with their people so that they could try our manufacturing process, visit the archives, see the dialogue of the company with the artworks. I guess they spotted the authenticity of our intentions, the importance of the factory as an organizational space that deserved our full dedication and pride. I am also welcoming companies who are interested in the production process and in how it is intertwined with the project of the archives and with living artists.

The Artists

The artists have been considered stakeholders in this process, especially in light of the idea that the project could develop emotions to work around the identity of the company and of the brand, and open it to a wider consideration of its stakeholders. Considering artists as stakeholders imply that their own emotions in the process are valued, as much as the empathy and pride that could develop among the artists themselves. This stakeholder approach to the artists can be devised in the willingness of the company to keep this first project as informal as possible to guarantee to the artists the needed freedom and creativity and, at the same time, a clear context where to operate. In addition, the company excluded a utilitarian and exploitative approach of artists' work, by avoiding formulating expectations in terms of their "performance." As the CEO explained:

> At least now, I want this more like a laboratory, than like an academy or an art foundation. I really think that this first attempt worked out very well, because everyone involved interpreted the experience like experimenting with something, which is not completely extraneous to us and it is not completely us at the same time. When the three artists entered the company, I sincerely did not know what I was going to expect from them and from the employees (…). I did not want a corporate approach to this, where 'communication' and 'reputation' are the key words. I did not have a so specific aim, I figured out the implications of what we were doing along the process.

Discussion and Implications

The intention of this exploratory study has been to start addressing how artification through artistic interventions can contribute to enriching stakeholder relations and clarifying brand identity in an authentic manner, specifically in the luxury fashion industry, which has had an active but limited relationship with the artistic interventions. The responses from the interviews and written survey support the notion that artification by engaging with artists and artworks in a company can stimulate meaningful conversations on themes that are not usually addressed at work: about shared values relating to the organization's origins, production process, the product, and the embeddedness of the company in its local context.

The case illustrates how artistic interventions are able to support employees in the process of identity work, by providing them with the perception of authenticity of the company and brand identity (Carroll, 2015). The case also illustrates how artistic interventions pushed the company to live and discuss its own identity considering a wider set of stakeholders than the fashion industry generally tends to do. In summary, these findings indicate that there are indeed good reasons for CSR scholars to consider corporate engagement with the arts beyond a philanthropic activity—although philanthropy doubtless remains a crucial role of companies in society today.

To enhance CSR research in this direction, we recommend drawing on strands of literature that has not yet been connected with CSR, namely, artification and organizational aesthetics (Gagliardi, 2006; Strati, 2000). Particularly, organizational aesthetics would enable CSR researchers to consider the diverse emotions stakeholders experience in relation to the organization, its product and production processes, and its identity. The emotional responses in the Sergio Rossi case include words like "excited," "blessed," "intrigued," "curious," "important," and they convey an overall sense that the process has been experienced as authentic and its outcomes as meaningful. Of course other disciplines, specifically psychology, also address emotions, but the advantage of aesthetic theories is that they incorporate bodies and materiality as well, which are central to experiences with the arts.

The data collected suggest that the experience in this company has been extremely positive. The question arises as to which features are likely to have led to such an outcome. Findings in previous research suggest that the active but non-instrumental engagement of top management throughout the process is a crucial component (Berthoin Antal et al., 2017). Of similar importance is the choice of an intermediary, in this case a curator, who knows the art world and is able to bridge between the logic and culture of the company with those of the arts (Berthoin Antal, 2016b). The choice of artists with a real interest in exploring the organization is of course a very significant factor. Further research would be needed in the organization to understand the dynamics more deeply.

This study has plausibly demonstrated the value of exploring the potential for addressing brand identity and CSR with multiple stakeholders in a fashion company in Italy. In order to advance the field, more cases would be needed in the fashion industry and in other sectors. For instance, it would be worth investigating whether there is a special aspect about the artisanship of the world of high fashion that is particularly important and what might be equivalent features in other sectors. In addition, given that the luxury fashion industry is more used to artistic collaborations on product and branding strategies, based on this explorative study it would be important to unpack how changing the way a company relates to art might affect employees' and stakeholders' perception of the company identity. Furthermore, it would be worth exploring whether a special attention to the sustainability of the world of luxury that can foster the presence of artists at the workplace and that can be compared to other dynamics in different sectors. Finally, given the cultural embeddedness of CSR and corporate cultures, it would be necessary to conduct comparative studies in other countries as well.

References

Balmer, J. M. T. (2008). Identity based views of the corporation: Insights from corporate identity, organisational identity, social identity, visual identity, corporate brand identity and corporate image. *European Journal of Marketing, 42*(9), 879–906.

Barry, D., & Meisiek, S. (2010). Sensemaking, mindfulness and the workarts: Seeing more and seeing differently. *Organization Studies, 31*(11), 1505–1530.

Baumgarth, C. (2018). Brand management and the world of the arts: Collaboration, co-operation, co-creation, and inspiration. *Journal of Product & Brand Management, 27*(3), 237–248.

Berthoin Antal, A. (2014). When arts enter organizational spaces: Implications for organizational learning. In A. Berthoin Antal, P. Meusburger, & L. Suarsana (Eds.), *Learning organizations: Extending the field* (pp. 177–201). Dordrecht, The Netherlands: Springer.

Berthoin Antal, A. (2016a). Artistic interventions in organizations: Beyond the fad. In A. R. Örtenblad (Ed.), *Handbook of research on management ideas and panaceas: Adaptation and context* (pp. 320–337). Cheltenham, UK and Northampton, MA: Edward Elgar.

Berthoin Antal, A. (2016b). The studio in the firm: A study of four artistic intervention residencies. In I. Farías & A. Wilkie (Eds.), *Studio studies: Operations, sites, displacements* (pp. 171–186). Abingdon, UK and New York, USA: Routledge.

Berthoin Antal, A., Debucquet, G., & Frémeaux, S. (2017). Leadership insights from artistic interventions in organizations. *Journal of Management Inquiry, 28*(4), 441–457.

Berthoin Antal, A., & Nussbaum-Bitran, I. (2015). *Artistic interventions in organizations: Data reports from multi-stakeholder surveys in Spain 2011–2014* (Discussion Paper SP III 2015-603). Wissenschaftszentrum Berlin für Sozialforschung. Retrieved November 1, 2019, from https://bibliothek.wzb.eu/pdf/2015/iii15-603.pdf.

Berthoin Antal, A., & Nussbaum Bitran, I. (2019). Discovering the meaningfulness of art in organizations: Experiences with add art Hamburg 2015. *Zeitschrift Für Kulturmanagement, 18*(2), 55–76.

Berthoin Antal, A., & Sobczak, A. (2004). Beyond CSR: Organizational learning for global responsibility. *Journal of General Management, 30*(2), 77–98.

Berthoin Antal, A., & Strauß, A. (2016). Multistakeholder perspectives on searching for evidence of values-added in artistic interventions in organizations. In U. Johansson Sköldberg, J. Woodilla, & A. Berthoin Antal (Eds.), *Artistic interventions in organizations: Research, theory and practice* (pp. 37–60). Abingdon, UK and New York, NY: Routledge.

Bessière, J. (2013). *Transformer l'organisation avec l'art. Etude retrospective pour évaluer l'impact résiduel dans le temps des démarches artistiques sur l'organisation. Le cas d'Eurogroup Consulting* (Unpublished Master thesis). Université Paris Dauphine, France.

Beverland, M. (2006). The 'real thing': Branding authenticity in the luxury wine trade. *Journal of Business Research, 59*(2), 251–258.

Brown, A. D., & Starkey, K. (2000). Organizational identity and learning: A psychodynamic perspective. *Academy of Management Review, 25*(1), 102–120.

Carroll, A. B. (1979). A three dimensional model of corporate social performance. *Academy of Management Review, 4*(3), 497–505.

Carroll, A. B. (1999). Corporate social responsibility—Evolution of a definitional construct. *Business and Society, 38*(3), 268–295.

Carroll, G. R. (2015). Authenticity: Attribution, value, and meaning. In A. R. Scott & S. M. Kosslyn (Eds.), *Emerging trends in the social and behavioral sciences: An interdisciplinary, searchable, and linkable resource* (pp. 1–13). Wiley.

Carù, A., Ostillio, M. C., & Leone, G. (2017). Corporate museums to enhance brand authenticity in luxury goods companies: The case of Salvatore Ferragamo. *International Journal of Arts Management, 19*(2), 32–45.

Creswell, J. (1994). *Research design: Qualitative and quantitative approaches.* London and New Delhi: Sage.

Darsø, L. (2004). *Artful creation: Learning-tales of arts-in-business.* Frederiksberg, DK: Samfundslitteratur.

Gagliardi, P. (2006). Exploring the aesthetic side of organizational life. In S. R. Clegg, C. Hardy, T. B. Lawrence, & W. R. Nord (Eds.), *The SAGE handbook of organization studies* (pp. 701–724). London: Sage.

Garriga, E., & Melé, D. (2004). Corporate social responsibility theories: Mapping the territory. *Journal of Business Ethics, 53*(1–2), 51–71.

Kapferer, J.-N. (2012). Abundant rarity: The key to luxury growth. *Business Horizons, 55*(5), 453–462.

Lewandowska, K. (2015). From sponsorship to partnership in arts and business relations. *The Journal of Arts Management, Law, and Society, 45*(1), 33–50.

Masè, S., & Cedrola, E. (2017). Louis Vuitton's art-based strategy to communicate exclusivity and prestige. In B. E. Jin & E. Cedrola (Eds.), *Fashion branding and communication* (pp. 155–184). New York: Palgrave Pivot.
Masè, S., & Silchenko, K. (2017). The Prada trend: Brand building at the intersection of design, art, technology, and retail experience. In B. E. Jin & E. Cedrola (Eds.), *Fashion branding and communication* (pp. 125–153). New York: Palgrave Pivot.
Paolino, C. (2019a). Il valore delle collezioni per la vita (anche sociale) dell'impresa. L'autenticità, la corporate social responsibility e i pubblici di riferimento dei musei e degli archivi d'impresa [The value of corporate collections for company (also social) performance. Authenticity, CSR and the audience of company museums and archives]. *Economia della Cultura, 1,* 6–31.
Paolino, C. (2019b). *Le corporate collection in Italia: dalla ricerca alla prassi* [*Corporate Collection in Italy: From research to practice*]. Bologna: Il Mulino.
Paolino, C., Smarrelli, M., & Carè, D. (2018). *Innovare l'impresa con l'arte: Il metodo della Fondazione Ermanno Casoli* [*Renewing companies through art: The methodology of Fondazione Ermanno Casoli*]. Milano: EGEA.
Strati, A. (2000). The aesthetic approach in organization studies. In S. Linstead & H. Höpfl (Eds.), *The aesthetics of organization* (pp. 13–34). London: Sage.
Waddock, S. (2004). Parallel universes: Companies, academics, and the progress of corporate citizenship. *Business and Society Review, 109*(1), 15–42.
Wood, D. J. (1991). Corporate social performance revisited. *Academy of Management Review, 16*(4), 691–718.

3

Trussardi Art and Fashion: A Long-Distance Relationship?

Andrea Rurale and Stefano Prestini

Abstract This chapter deals with the artification strategies developed by Trussardi, a renowned Italian luxury fashion brand. Trussardi represents an illustrative example of a formal separation between Trussardi art foundation and luxury fashion brand that counterintuitively leads in a positive authentic contamination between art and fashion from the consumers point of view. Indeed, through the analysis of secondary data and an exclusive interview with Beatrice Trussardi, the President of the Trussardi Foundation, this chapter investigates the idiosyncratic dichotomy between the company—the Trussardi Fashion *Maison*—and the Nicola Trussardi Foundation—an institution aimed at the promotion of contemporary art. By outlining the main findings, this chapter aims

A. Rurale (✉) · S. Prestini
Bocconi University, Milan, Italy
e-mail: rurale@unibocconi.it

S. Prestini
e-mail: stefano.prestini@unibocconi.it

M. Massi and A. Turrini (eds.), *The Artification of Luxury Fashion Brands*, Palgrave Studies in Practice: Global Fashion Brand Management,
https://doi.org/10.1007/978-3-030-26121-4_3

to clearly identify the distinct origins and developments of both realities, thus eliciting the positive externalities of the two separated entities.

Keywords Art foundations · Art & brand contaminations · Authenticity, contemporary art, legitimization

Introduction

The luxury goods market is constantly increasing, and 2018 was no exception. Indeed, the overall luxury market—including both luxury goods and experiences—grew by 5% in 2018, at persistent exchange rates, to reach an estimated value of €1.2 trillion globally (D'Arpizio, Levato, Prete, Del Fabbro, & de Montgolfier, 2019). Though this positive performance is evident throughout the luxury market, the personal luxury goods segment in particular, which includes luxury fashion brands, outclassed the market in 2018, maintaining a 6% growth and reaching a €260 billion turnover. This incremental development is estimated to continue, in the range of 3–5% per year, through 2025, according to the Bain Luxury Study (D'Arpizio et al., 2019).

In this positive trend, art meaningfully influences relationships with luxury brands, particularly luxury fashion brands. Fashion historian Valerie Steele differentiates between fashion (an industry with a creative element, a commodity with a commercial nature) and art (a field of high cultural production, including sculptures, paintings, and music associated with a greater aesthetic realm) (Steele, 2012). However, the luxury market has made the relationships between art and fashion evident in various ways. Today, the borders separating luxury fashion, art and consumption are particularly fluid. This amalgamation, elicited by discourses, associations and creative correlations, has come to be seen as a traditional connection and, over the years, has resulted in a commercially lucrative relationship (Gregory, 2014). Extant literature has offered examples of this connection between luxury and art in various ways, such as luxury brands offering financial support for art events, luxury fashion designers collaborating with artists, luxury fashion exhibitions in museums and galleries and fashion shows becoming more similar to live art performances (Codignola & Rancati, 2016). There are also luxury fashion designers who set themselves in exquisitely artistic environments and see themselves as artists, making this affiliation identifiable throughout brand identity (Smith, Kubler, & Guinness, 2013). On the one side, there are luxury collections—e.g., Martin Margiela, Hussein Chalayan, and Alexander McQueen—with social and political messages merging fashion and art (Twist, 2005). On the other side, there are collections purposely using art as a pure marketing strategy to elevate brand image and develop competitive advantage—e.g., Louis Vuitton (Jelinek, 2018).

This chapter considers Trussardi—that is, the Trussardi Fashion Company and the Nicola Trussardi Foundation. Trussardi's fashion segment, with Tomaso Trussardi as its current CEO, reported sales of more than €20 million in 2018. The brand has an almost global presence, with its Trussardi and Trussardi Jeans lines, and has a large portfolio of licensing lines, including furniture, perfumes, and eyewear. The company has over 160 boutiques in Italy, Europe and Asia. In addition to its online store at Trussardi.com, the label is carried by more than 1800 multi-brand and department stores (La Stampa, 2019). On the other side, the Nicola Trussardi Foundation is an institution for promoting contemporary art and is autonomous from its namesake, the Trussardi Luxury Fashion Maison. The present research investigates this iconic autonomy between the Trussardi art foundation and the Trussardi luxury brand, which, counterintuitively, has led to positive contamination of the founder's shared values into both organizations. The authors describe the development paths of both segments and elicit the potential externalities of this (non)relationship.

The chapter is organized as follows. First, it presents an overview of the company and provides the rationale for studying the Trussardi case. Second, it describes the history of the Trussardi Maison. Third, it presents the Trussardi art and fashion contamination—particularly illustrating the fruitful, indirect connection between the Trussardi Luxury Fashion Maison and the Nicola Trussardi Foundation as an idiosyncratic, contamination-based (non)relationship, which indirectly links the brand with art. Fourth, the chapter outlines and discusses the positive externalities and synergies between the two business segments, contributing to extant artification literature by demonstrating a different approach to managing and developing an art foundation generated in a luxury fashion company context. Finally, the authors identify managerial implications and conclude the chapter by offering potential steps for future research.

Company Overview

The Trussardi Luxury Fashion Maison is one of the most successful businesses in the global accessories market. It is, historically, a family-owned business and is currently facing change—ceding control to an asset management company ahead of brand relaunch. Tomaso Trussardi will remain chairman of the board, representing the heritage of the Trussardi family. The company's strategy focuses on the Trussardi heritage, luxurious and crafted leather goods, and products made in Italy, as well as potential "brand extensions," such as its perfume partnership with the Angelini Group (La Stampa, 2019).

Trussardi's global dimension is represented by the 47 countries in which it is present through both the Trussardi and Trussardi Jeans lines. As mentioned above, the Trussardi Luxury Fashion Maison contains a large portfolio of licensing lines, including furniture, perfumes, and eyewear, and is currently also creating a partnership with the automotive industry. With a creative and innovative marketing campaign, Trussardi and Fiat Chrysler Automobiles (FCA) launched, in 2019, the "Panda Trussardi," a car with an Italian urban-chic DNA. Trussardi's 160 boutiques in Italy, Europe and Asia are integrated by ecommerce at Trussardi.com, the company's numerical coverage is globally represented by more than 1800 points-of-sale in both multi-brand and department stores.

According to the last Statista report on Trussardi (2019), the company generated sales of more than €20.32 million euros in 2018. This amount illustrates an increasing trend in turnover after 2014, when revenues were at their lowest for the 2011–2018 period (see Fig. 3.1).

Concerning profit and loss, Trussardi's financial situation shows that the company has been facing a change, during which some relevant allowances created negative profit results (see Fig. 3.2). This challenging

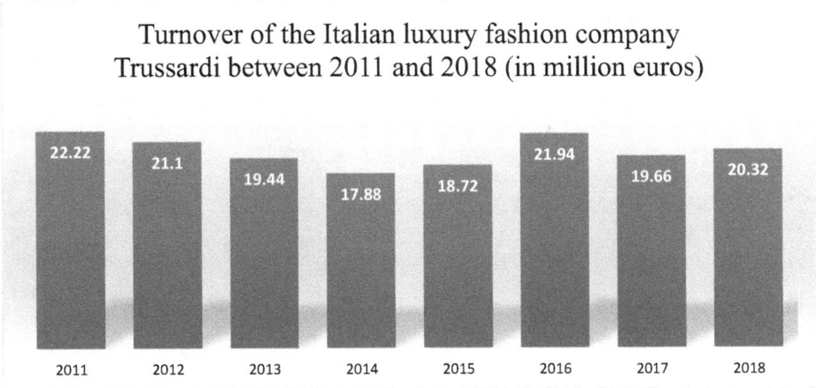

Fig. 3.1 Trussardi turnovers 2011–2018 (*Source* Developed by the authors based on Statista and Trussardi financial statement data)

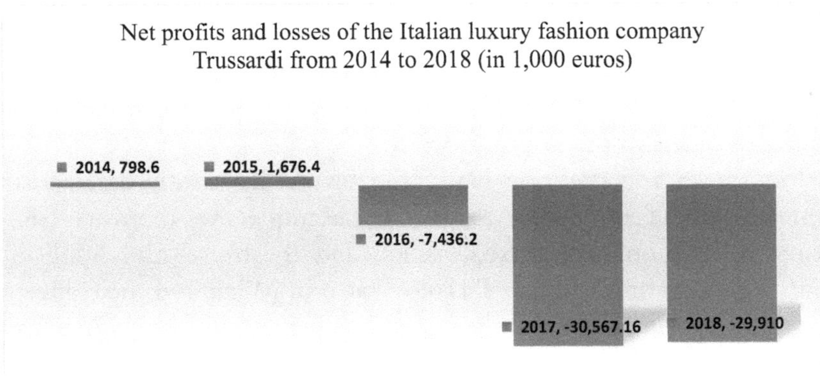

Fig. 3.2 Trussardi profits and losses, 2014–2018 (*Source* Developed by the authors based on Statista and Trussardi financial statement data)

period led Trussardi to focus on brand repositioning, such as the concept store 'T' Trussardi', which represents a mix of contemporaneity and tradition.

Although profits suffered in the last period due to financial issues, Trussardi's number of employees is still increasing to satisfy market demands for the unique Trussardi experience (Fig. 3.3). Therefore, the company has translated its culture into deeper market development in,

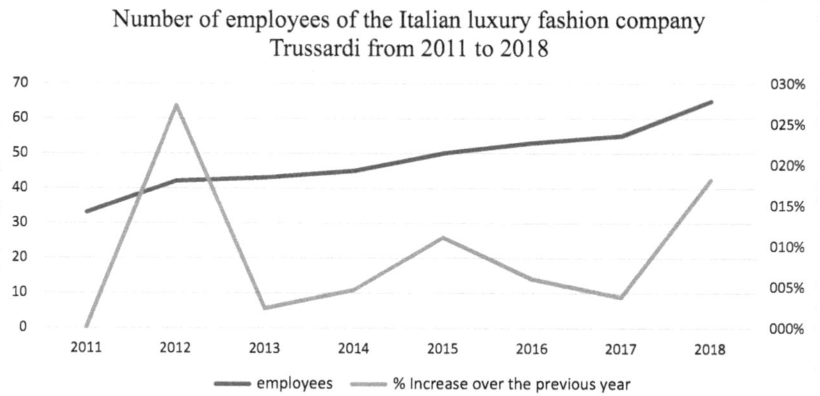

Fig. 3.3 Trussardi employees, 2011–2018 (*Source* Developed by the authors based on Statista and Trussardi financial statement data)

for example, Asia and the Middle East. It has opened new single-brand boutiques in Hong Kong, Moscow, and Taiwan, and created new, innovative store concepts, like the T-Store—a unique, modular space housing all the products in the Trussardi world.

Innovation and tradition have been pivotal Trussardi characteristics representing the company's strengths. For example, over the years, Nicola Trussardi harmoniously mixed fashion and theatre, costume and customs, collaborating with the Piccolo Teatro in Milan and their director, Giorgio Strehler. He dressed the cast of Macbeth at the Verona Arena and staged a fashion show at Sforza Castle with the extraordinary direction of Dario Argento. Advertising campaigns were also deployed at this time to publicize the Trussardi style all over the world, especially through collaborations with top international photographers, like Richard Avedon, Mario Testino, Michel Comte, and Steven Klein. This artistic sensitivity eventually led to the creation of the Nicola Trussardi Foundation for contemporary art, which currently represents some of the most relevant Italian and international artists in the contemporary scene. Additionally, hearkening to the photography campaigns during Nicola Trussardi's tenure, an innovative co-marketing campaign between Fiat Panda and Trussardi, featuring Ava Max's face and voice, will accompany the launch of Panda Trussardi. This integrated communication campaign has been signed by Independent Ideas and will be under the creative direction of Erick Loi.

Research also contributes to the current image of Trussardi's products and projects. For example, a legacy of the most refined leatherworking processes, combined with continuous research into new clothing and material manufacturing techniques, has put the brand at the center of new design and fashion trends internationally. Trussardi's creativity is a DNA component of the company, which now, as in the past, has been reinventing and updating itself consistently. However, Trussardi never leaves its contemporary vision, which always distinguishes its founder, the company and its foundation.

Trussardi's attitude of leveraging on innovation and creativity—represented by contemporary marketing campaigns, strong traditional and familiar roots and the natural integration of art and creativity—called for further analysis to understand how the company represents art and luxury contamination. Trussardi has, in fact, been associated with many cultural events and contemporary art installations because of the Nicola Trussardi Foundation. Therefore, the goal of this chapter is to understand the potential art and luxury contamination strategy characterizing the Trussardi world.

Company History

In 1911, Dante Trussardi founded Trussardi in Bergamo, Italy, as a workshop producing and distributing luxury gloves. Nicola Trussardi made the Trussardi group one of the most successful in the global accessories market, and it was appointed official supplier to the British royal family.

In the 1960s, Nicola Trussardi brought the company's leather goods production to a new level, combining quality materials with cutting-edge design and leatherworking research. This kickstarted the production of bags, suitcases, and home accessories, establishing the first real foundations of what was soon to become the quintessential Italian lifestyle brand.

In 1973, Trussardi became the first fashion Maison to use a symbol to identify all its products: the greyhound, representing agility and dynamism. In 1976, the first Trussardi boutique opened on Via Sant'Andrea in Milan.

The revolution continued in the 1980s, when Trussardi launched its ready-to-wear collection, forging special partnerships with some of the most admired Italian brands, such as Alfa Romeo, Alitalia, Garelli and Agusta, and consolidating its reputation as a symbol of the truly authentic Italian style. In 1984, Trussardi surprised the public by choosing an uncommon location for its autumn/winter women's collection fashion show: Piazza del Duomo, Milan. This made Trussardi the first brand in the world to take fashion away from more "exclusive" locations and open it to wider audiences by hosting public fashion shows.

In 1996, Trussardi alla Scala opened in one of the most iconic locations in Milan, given its proximity to Teatro alla Scala. It was the first flagship building in the fashion world to house, not only a showroom and boutique, but also a space dedicated to a café and a restaurant. Beatrice Trussardi, daughter of Nicola Trussardi and Chair of the Nicola Trussardi Foundation, says of this endeavor: "*It was an example of the idea of [giving] back to the city of Milan.... The idea was to create to stimulate [the] exchange of cultural meanings [from] which not only [the] fashion world could benefit but also a wider audience*" (Interview with Beatrice Trussardi, 2019).

Artification Strategy

Trussardi represents an instance of contamination between art and a luxury fashion brand. In the Trussardi case, what is driving the contamination between art and the brand is the Nicola Trussardi Foundation, an organization committed to "the transmission and dissemination of culture" (Fondazione Nicola Trussardi, 2020). Establishing a foundation is a common artification strategy aimed to improve a fashion brand's image and reputation. Many companies that have established their own foundations to enhance their brand—e.g., Louis Vuitton, Gucci, Gianfranco Ferré, Cartier, Hermes, Ermenegildo Zegna, and Prada. This strategic integration has been particularly evident for Prada, which consistently sets some of its luxury fashion shows inside the Prada Foundation. Such events publicly stress the association between the art foundation and the luxury fashion Maison, enhancing and benefitting from the aura of authenticity and exclusivity brought about by an art-based context. A foundation can function as a brand extension—a culture-driven subject—of the luxury fashion company. Indeed, the extant literature regards foundations as optimal tools for improving brand-related experiences through the experience economy (Pine & Gilmore, 1999). Thus, foundations generated by luxury fashion Maisons are often expressions of a purely commercial interest in art (Smith et al., 2013).

However, this is not what emerges in the idiosyncratic relationship between the Nicola Trussardi Foundation and the Trussardi Fashion Maison. In both contexts, issues of separation and autonomy are counterintuitively stressed, while potential connections are not explicitly outlined. Therefore, this chapter investigates why this commitment to autonomy exists and explores the underpinning contaminations between the Trussardi segments, as well as the benefits of this (non)relationship. The following section presents the Nicola Trussardi Foundation, illustrating how this cultural organization expresses the vision of Nicola Trussardi, whose values authentically emerged, both in the luxury company and in the contemporary art foundation. These two segments of Trussardi are also separately managed, and this must be examined to fully understand the positive effects of the long-distance contamination between art and luxury.

The Nicola Trussardi Foundation: Positive Externalities of a Long-Distance Contamination

Founded in Milan in 1996, the Nicola Trussardi Foundation is a non-profit institution for promoting contemporary culture. Neither a museum nor a collection, the Trussardi Foundation acts as an agency for producing and diffusing contemporary art in a wide variety of contexts and channels. Beatrice Trussardi explains: "*Contemporary artists are the thinkers of today*" (Interview with Beatrice Trussardi, 2019).

As an example, Trussardi alla Scala, in particular, showcased Trussardi's vision of combining art and luxury—creating synergy among different cultural disciplines and relations between luxury and art. As Beatrice Trussardi put it, "*...a person could buy luxury, fashion, but also a book in the bookshop or have lunch in the cafeteria, conceived as a museum café*" (Interview with Beatrice Trussardi, 2019). Trussardi alla Scala boasted a space for exhibitions—theatre, figurative art, music, etc.,—and "*[a] common note was innovation, the particular detail that was always present in the artistic and cultural expression of Nicola Trussardi. This was the genesis of the foundation*" (Interview with Beatrice Trussardi, 2019).

In recent years, the Nicola Trussardi Foundation has established partnerships with municipal governments, national public institutions and other prestigious international institutions, museums and exhibitions, such as the Tate Modern in London, the Kunsthaus in Zurich and the Venice Biennale.

Originating when the Maison and foundation were strongly related, the Nicola Trussardi Foundation evolved toward a more independent and autonomous path, achieved through contamination. Its place, in the center of Milan, hosted several exhibitions every year, but the distance between the broad audience and the exclusive contemporary art exhibitions pushed Beatrice Trussardi in a new direction. In 2002, she appointed Massimiliano Gioni as artistic director. In January 2003, after many years of activity in the exhibition spaces of Palazzo Marino alla Scala, the Nicola Trussardi Foundation began exploring new territories and modes of displaying contemporary art, pushing the boundaries of the spaces traditionally devoted to contemporary creativity.

Since then, the foundation has changed its brand positioning, becoming, as Beatrice Trussardi explains, "*an agency of production of contemporary arts, unique projects where the container is deeply connected and interrelated with the content*" (Interview with Beatrice Trussardi, 2019). Thus, the venues for the foundation's projects become part of the artistic creation itself. The foundation seeks out secluded parts of Milan to make them, alongside contemporary art installations, known by wider audiences, with no need to pay for tickets. Beatrice Trussardi explains: "*The Foundation is hosted in places which do not belong to us but that we help make available and known by the public*" (Interview with Beatrice Trussardi, 2019).

Over the years, the Nicola Trussardi Foundation has deliberately increased its distance from the Trussardi Luxury Fashion Maison to such an extent that Beatrice Trussardi talks about "*two geneses*" (Interview with Beatrice Trussardi, 2019). The first occurred in 1996 with the inauguration of the Trussardi Palace (in Piazza della Scala, Milan) and the formal constitution of the Nicola Trussardi Foundation. The second occurred in 2003, when the foundation left the building in Piazza della Scala: "*This was the main reason why I left the Piazza della Scala office because it was perceived as an elitist place for the few or for those who are already experts*" (Interview with Beatrice Trussardi, 2019). In fact, the idea Beatrice Trussardi had in mind was to introduce contemporary art to Milan, which, 2003, was perceived as irrelevant: "*Most people did not know contemporary artists. Here came the need to make it clear that anybody can see an exhibition of contemporary art and understand the cutting-edge innovation that the Foundation always wanted to convey. The Trussardi Foundation also aimed to make it clear that contemporary art exists and that it has something to say. As well as you read a book or listen to contemporary music, you can be exposed to contemporary art. Obviously, in these 16 years, the city has evolved fortunately [...] and so now we also emphasise other missions related to our activity: we want to talk about global, crucial, fundamental topics for our society through artistic projects*" (Interview with Beatrice Trussardi, 2019).

An Exclusive Relationship

The distance the Nicola Trussardi Foundation has been taking from the Trussardi Luxury Fashion Maison becomes even more significant considering that luxury brands tend to exclusivity, not inclusion (Radon, 2012). Exclusivity is one reason why the Trussardi Foundation and the Trussardi luxury brand are separated. If, in general, exclusivity is well expressed by both art and luxury, the Trussardi Foundation's vision is to convey art to everyone based on a perspective of art democratization. Such democratization would be difficult for a luxury brand to manage, since it must ideally aim to target high-spending consumers. Nevertheless, art does embody the construct of rarity (expressed by each piece's uniqueness), which is also one of the most iconic characteristics of luxury. For luxury firms, art market commercial organizations traditionally ensure rarity by limiting an artist's production or an artwork's editions. Extraordinariness is another concept connected to rarity (Kapferer, 2012). Both for luxury fashion brands and artworks, it refers to the expert segment, which often interferes with determining stylistic or artistic trends (Codignola & Rancati, 2016).

Codignola and Rancati (2016) analyze the birth of contemporary art foundations established by top luxury fashion brands, determining that, if the increasingly common strategic relationship between luxury fashion brands and art continues to grow, the luxury fashion industry, along with its top brand-driven foundations, will be forced to change the structure and dynamics between brands and homonymous foundations. To promote their brands, luxury fashion managers are already becoming increasingly conscious of the commercial power behind creating new, contemporary forms of expressions and innovative initiatives.

As Codignola and Rancati (2016) state, "[t]he sustained development of luxury fashion firms challenges the foundation of a luxury fashion brand that should be implicitly exclusive. The mass production of fashioned goods represents a considerable variable that threatens brand exclusivity, brand valorization, and brand impression" (p. 55). Kapferer (2012) observes that, to pursue "exclusivity," a brand must account for the implicit contradictions in luxury branding—maintaining scarcity while pursuing market growth and expansion. Thus, luxury fashion firms and brands acting in a global context must deal with market dynamics that regularly contradict exclusivity (Codignola & Rancati, 2016).

However, as in the luxury fashion industry, there has been a shift in the art world. Today's proliferation of museums, art events, and art fairs has transformed the art world into a collection of mass spaces where, despite its "uniqueness" and "exclusivity," art can be approached or consumed by almost everyone. Such a fact, conversely, means that "the status of art itself has drastically changed in society, so that creation has become endowed with prestige" (Kapferer, 2014, p. 375). The contemporary art market is increasingly dominated by fashionable players, from celebrity collectors to celebrity artists or celebrity museums. Consequently, society celebrates it as the latest glittering, global playground, perfectly suiting the richest global consumers. Desires for emulation are widespread, exactly as they are for luxury goods, where owning a status symbol is the primary stimulus. The art world has always been a field of desire, aspiration, and seduction, in part because the art market creates and distributes goods that have more of a symbolic, rather than material, value (Codignola & Rancati, 2016).

From this perspective, the Nicola Trussardi Foundation differs from a corporate museum, as described by Carù, Ostillio, and Leone (2017), who investigate corporate museums as tools for enriching brand authenticity. Traditionally, corporate museums have focused on company history, underlining the contributions of founders and other key individuals and displaying historical documents, photographs, and products. Nissley and Casey (2002) broaden the scope of corporate museums to include a form of organizational memory strategically used to develop firm and brand identity and image. The Nicola Trussardi Foundation is completely autonomous from the original Maison, with which it only shares its name and basic values that "*can be traced back to the identity of Nicola Trussardi*" (Interview with Beatrice Trussardi, 2019). The effective independence of the Nicola Trussardi Foundation from the Trussardi Luxury Fashion Maison is maintained by clear distinctions of activities (e.g., no collaborations between the organizations), different governance, distant headquarters, no shared spaces and different brands and logos. The Nicola Trussardi Foundation's activities are financially supported by the three founding members—Beatrice, Maria Luisa, and Gaia Trussardi—with the aid of a group of private patrons, who believe in the foundation's cultural model and mission. In specific cultural initiatives, companies and other institutions offer further financial aid. These characteristics of clear independence are quite unique compared to other foundations generated in the luxury context, in which relationships are much more evident and prominent. For example, the Prada Foundation is based in front of one of the fashion company's sites (in Via Orobia, Milan), and it hosted Prada's spring 2019 women's fashion show in its theatre. The Louis Vuitton Foundation is another example of evident collaboration and dependence between foundation and luxury house.

Louis Vuitton fashion shows have been organized in the Louis Vuitton Foundation (e.g., the spring 2015 fashion show), and the Louis Vuitton brand sponsors the foundation. The Gucci Museum offers another case of conspicuous collaboration and influence. It dedicates a large part of its cultural offering to exploring the Gucci story and the brand's most iconic fashion pieces (e.g., the room of handbags).

Although Trussardi has wished to separate its foundation from its fashion Maison, both are, historically and presently, based on the founding characteristics of the Trussardi brand. Beyond the product, the brand has its own history, memory, and traditions: "*These aspects are fundamental, and we must constantly confront [them] when we produce the new, be it art or luxury*" (Interview with Beatrice Trussardi, 2019). This has been the Nicola Trussardi Foundation's attitude in its work with the historical places of Milan, "*being able to talk about today and tomorrow through contemporary art projects*" (Interview with Beatrice Trussardi, 2019).

Therefore, despite their differences and calculated separation, the foundation and the Maison share common ground: "*the farsightedness, the unpredictability, of unexpected, disruptive creation (both luxury and art), which are common features that represent the figure of my father, Nicola Trussardi*" (Interview with Beatrice Trussardi, 2019). Thus, according to the shared values of Nicola Trussardi, the Nicola Trussardi Foundation and the Trussardi Fashion Company coexist and reinforce each other's values while maintaining their autonomy and distinct identities.

Discussion

When analyzing the idiosyncratic case of the Nicola Trussardi Foundation and the Trussardi Luxury Fashion Maison, various counterintuitive lessons emerge. The origins of the Trussardi Foundation demonstrate that, in its first period, it was integrated with the Trussardi Luxury Fashion Maison to benefit from the main advantages of the classic integration between art and luxury fashion brands. Indeed, coherently with the Nobbs, Moore, and Sheridan (2012), the foundation was in the Trussardi headquarters building, representing a way, not only to promote art, but also to increase the time shoppers spent in the flagship store, where they could experience art exhibitions, cafés and restaurants in a holistic and experiential approach.

Nicola Trussardi also enhanced the relationships between the two segments of the company, presenting the homonymous foundation as a way to thank Milan, which had given him many opportunities in the luxury fashion environment. In this sense, the Trussardi luxury brand could benefit from the magic aura of being an exclusive, creative, innovative and culturally driven fashion company, due to the foundation. These values were synergistically elicited in the explicit association between the Trussardi Foundation and the Trussardi brand. Brand heritage and authenticity were also prompted by this recognized connection. In fact, the role of the Trussardi family, and, in particular, of Nicola Trussardi, was the common pillar of both realities, embodying authenticity and heritage in these hand-in-hand worlds. Many foundations and museums in the luxury brand context currently represent this approach to the relationship between art and luxury (e.g., Salvatore Ferragamo) (Carù et al., 2017).

However, the Trussardi Foundation's performance results, in terms of numbers of visitors and resonance, were not remarkable. The role of the Trussardi Foundation was, in fact, secondary—under the aura of the better-known fashion Maison. Both physically and perceptively, the Trussardi Foundation was part of the luxury brand (as a brand extension). As mentioned previously, the Trussardi Foundation was confined to the part of the Trussardi headquarters that included the main flagship store. This integrated location implied that most foundation visitors were also current Trussardi shoppers. This led the foundation toward an unsolicited, élite approach that prefiltered the potential visitor numbers and hampered the resonance of the foundation's name. This limited the extent to which the contaminations between art and luxury could be exploited for both realities.

The 2003 "renaissance" of the Nicola Trussardi Foundation concretely represented a formal and substantial separation from its luxury fashion parent company. The foundation strongly expressed its independence, cutting explicit links with the luxury brand. The Trussardi Luxury Fashion Maison is not even the financial supporter of the foundation, nor is the foundation's governance involved in the fashion company's ownership. The foundation intended to leave the headquarters building looking for a "place" that better represented its autonomous identity. This place was Milan, and, in a "nomadic" approach, the foundation comes alive each time ad hoc art installations are placed in undiscovered locations of the Milanese area. The need for autonomy, in cohesion with the foundation's mission, was, and is, expressed through its producing and spreading contemporary art among a wide variety of contexts, channels, and people (via free exhibitions). This mission binds, in a strong, authentic way, the city of Milan to the foundation, which has been renovating different abandoned areas to install many indoor and outdoor artworks—thereby embodying the metaphor of the melted representation of innovation and tradition conveyed by the Nicola Trussardi DNA. The same fusion of tradition and innovation has been expressed by embracing the contemporary artworks incorporated and adapted in historical Milanese areas. The separation between the Nicola Trussardi Foundation and the Trussardi Luxury Fashion Maison clearly improved the Foundation's performance—increasing the number of visitors to the contemporary art exhibition and enhancing the resonance and awareness of the non-profit organization

However, is an art foundation's independent from its parent luxury brand better than integration? Why does this non-relationship provide positive effects, and what are its main outcomes? The positive outcomes the Nicola Trussardi Foundation experienced are coherent with recent research about brand prominence in marketing communication. If consumers observe a brand, conspicuously and frequently, through storytelling forms of communication, such as contemporary art exhibitions explicitly promoted by a luxury brand (even through its foundation), they will perceive the art as a tool for enhance sales of the brand's products. Consumers tend to respond negatively to such stories (Teixeira, Wedel, & Pieters, 2010). Therefore, many brands, which communicate through different channels, are now giving more relevance to the content and making the branding itself less prominent. This soft approach reduces consumers' perceptions of "sales tools" and is often conducive for engaging consumers with the content—the values told in the story.

In this case, an autonomous foundation serves as a way to transfer values, emotions, innovations, and creativity to a huge number of visitors in a more authentic and engaging way. Such is the case with the Nicola Trussardi Foundation. No elements related to the Trussardi Luxury Fashion Maison are voluntarily associated with the nomadic contemporary exhibitions (Teixeira et al., 2010), and no immediate ulterior business motives are displayed. This upstream choice expresses the authenticity current consumers ask from markets, across different industries, brands and profit and no-profit organizations. This experience of authenticity is strongly prevalent in art and luxury environments (Joy, Wang, Chan, Sherry, & Cui, 2014).

However, despite this independence, the two segments of Trussardi maintain some essential roots. The homonymous name, "Trussardi," hearkens to their shared founders. This indissoluble common basis represents their mutual origins and symbolizes a powerful source of distinctive values that differentiate the fashion brand and the foundation in the luxury and contemporary art contexts. Nicola Trussardi himself embodied tradition and innovation, legitimization and rarity, which nurtured both the brand and the foundation. These effects remain valid, though leadership is now in the hands of different members of the Trussardi family and the organizations follow different strategic developments. A founder always remains a major element of the authenticity for art foundations and luxury Maisons (Carù et al., 2017).

In this "long-distance relationship" between the Nicola Trussardi Foundation and the Trussardi Luxury Fashion Maison, Nicola Trussardi's vision and values must be constantly enhanced—particularly through the creation of contemporary art exhibitions. In this way, Nicola Trussardi's identity maintains its irreplaceable role, authentically expressing the values of both organizations. In this way, Nicola Trussardi becomes the central pillar, eliciting positive externalities for the foundation and the Maison. The major externalities of this "long-distance relationship" between art and luxury are the following:

- Tradition and innovation.
- Legitimization.
- Rarity and universality.

Each of these positive externalities is discussed in the following paragraphs.

Tradition and Innovation

"*We cross innovation and tradition in the fusion between contemporary art and territory*" (Interview with Beatrice Trussardi, 2019). Nicola Trussardi expressed an original mix of tradition and innovative vision in the luxury fashion context and the world of art exhibitions. This approach is currently embodied and boosted through the Nicola Trussardi Foundation and its contemporary art installations in Milanese historical areas. These visionary exhibitions are carefully laid metaphors of tradition and innovation, managed by foundation president Beatrice Trussardi and artistic director Massimiliano Gioni. Tradition is elicited from the foundation's connection with the Milanese territory, to which Nicola Trussardi was strongly attached, while innovation emerges through the ad hoc contemporary art installations inserted in selected Milanese areas. Tradition and innovation are vital, for both the foundation and the luxury brand (Jackson & Shaw, 2009; Okonkwo, 2007). Due to Nicola Trussardi's prominent role, the foundation and the fashion company benefit from his essential, distinctive values.

Legitimization

"*The founder – Nicola Trussardi – and his values represent the Foundation genesis and DNA that cannot be cancelled; indeed, they should be enhanced*" (Interview with Beatrice Trussardi, 2019). Luxury fashion brands greatly require legitimization because luxury companies must explain the high prices they charge for products, which often face accusations of being too expensive without a real reason. Therefore, luxury brand managers position their products as expressions of tradition and culture, art and creativity and timelessness (Kapferer, 2014). Connection with art is a precious association and strategy luxury companies use to enhance these legitimating values (Smith et al., 2013). However, as the Trussardi case shows, the connection between a luxury brand and its art foundation should not be brazenly communicated, as this could sacrifice consumer engagement (Teixeira et al., 2010). The legitimating link between luxury and art is more authentically transmitted through the founder, avoiding the risk of consumers perceiving purely commercial ulterior motives. The Trussardi brand is never shown during exhibitions, and the foundation is a non-profit organization, perpetuating Nicola Trussardi's values and artistic inspirations.

Rarity and Universality

The rarity principle suggests that, to maintain prestige, luxury brands must sustain high levels of awareness and tightly control brand diffusion to enhance exclusivity (Phau & Prendergast, 2000). Contextually, luxury brands must satisfy global, yet heterogeneous, demands from larger and newer markets (Codignola & Rancati, 2016). The Nicola Trussardi Foundation is a successful example of how this trade-off can be overcome through an indirect relationship. The Trussardi Luxury Fashion Maison benefits from the Nicola Trussardi Foundation through contamination—association with true expressions of contemporary art installations, which pursue the "democratization of art," making the art exhibitions free and open to a heterogeneous public.

On the one side, contemporary art is naturally open to highlighting the social issues that concern global audiences (e.g., the Restless Earth exhibition in 2017, which gave voice to immigrants and refugees). On the other side, all art exhibitions express rarity because they are temporary, totally unique and unrepeatable. Indeed, Trussardi art installations are inserted and created according to each selected place in Milan, which becomes an integral part of the artistic work. Here, again, these values of universality and rarity are enhanced for both the foundation and the brand, due to the identity of Nicola Trussardi, making these promoted values authentic for consumers. In sum, therefore, the authors propose that the Trussardi brand establishes a non-relationship with its foundation, with which it stays connected through indirect contamination processes (Fig. 3.4).

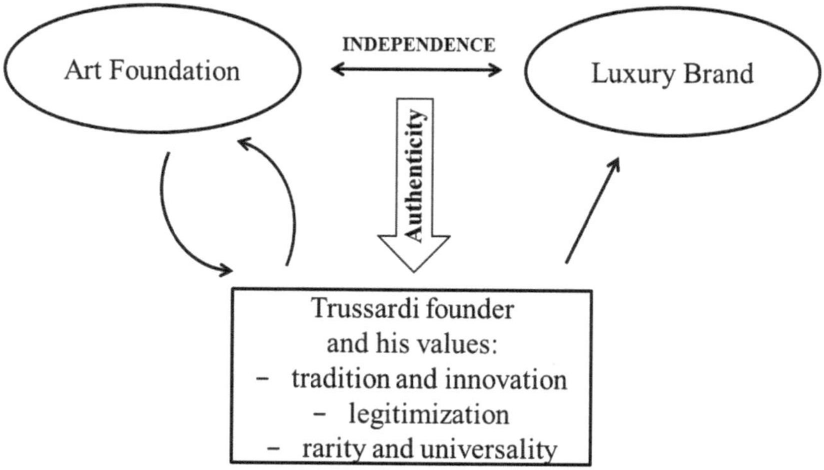

Fig. 3.4 The virtuous "long-distance relationship" model in the luxury-art contamination (*Source* Authors' elaboration)

In luxury fashion companies, which share founders with their related art foundations, a virtuous model emerges in the so-called "long-distance relationship" or "non-relationship." The Trussardi Foundation, through its contemporary art exhibitions, enhances the distinctive values of Nicola Trussardi. Consumers perceive these values as authentic due to the clear independence of the foundation from the Trussardi Luxury Fashion Maison. Indeed, as previously mentioned, the Nicola Trussardi Foundation is a distinctive entity from the Trussardi fashion company, with no collaboration between the two. The common, but pivotal, element is Nicola Trussardi and his values are maintained by both the organizations, constituting the DNA of the foundation and the company. In this way, people do not perceive the foundation as having ulterior strategical and secular motives to integrate art and luxury for business purposes. This approach is quite far from that employed by other foundations or museums in the luxury context, which conspicuously intertwine fashion shows in their foundations' spaces or artificate luxury objects (e.g., the Gucci Museum displaying iconic fashion pieces). Thus, the independence of the two Trussardi organizations creates positive contamination generated by Nicola Trussardi's values.

Nevertheless, how can Trussardi concretely maintain this autonomy while benefiting from these positive externalities? To show, and help consumers perceive, the separation between the foundation and the luxury brand, Trussardi elicits some operational elements that enhance this autonomy, while retaining the positive association with those essential values.

First, an art foundation headquarters should be in a different location away from any of its fashion company's touchpoints. Fashion and luxury businesses must maintain, both perceptually and physically, the correct distance to express authentic independence. In the Trussardi case, the art foundation is present, in a nomadic way, in the city of Milan, while the Trussardi Luxury Fashion Maison has kept its headquarter in Piazza della Scala.

Second, the tone of voice adopted by an art foundation and its fashion Maison in their image, communications, and logos must be evidently independent. Neither party should mention the other when discussing their various activities. Websites, advertisements and institutional communications should use autonomous tones of voice to maintain a clear independence.

The final determining factor is that different leadership must be appointed in each organization to maintain real autonomy and avoid business market trends that could influence cultural and artistic offerings or the foundation's values. In the Trussardi case, Beatrice Trussardi serves as the president of the Nicola Trussardi Foundation, while Tomaso Trussardi and Quattro R own the Trussardi Luxury Fashion Maison.

In the following section, the authors will highlight the main contributions of this research to the extant literature and will discuss some managerial implications the study has for luxury fashion companies that have been integrating art into their organizations.

Conclusion and Implications

This chapter has dealt with Trussardi as an example of the artification of a luxury brand, which has mainly occurred through the existence of two distinct bodies contaminating each other—the Nicola Trussardi Foundation and the Trussardi Luxury Fashion Maison. It would be expected that, if a luxury fashion company desires to embrace art as a method of enhancing its image and positioning, the luxury Maison should stress this connection as much as possible. However, counterintuitively, current consumers would disengage from art offered as a conspicuous ploy for brand prominence. Instead, consumers look for authentic content and products (Teixeira et al., 2010). The Nicola Trussardi Foundation does not include or involve any fashion-related activities in its cultural offerings. The situation is significantly different in most other foundations, where company influence on the foundations is prominent and the intertwined activities are more evident (e.g., Prada and Louis Vuitton fashion shows inside their respective art foundations, the presence of fashion pieces in the Gucci Museum and financial support of the LVMH group on the Louis Vuitton Foundation). Therefore, the authors suggest that art foundations' management should enhance their independence from their parent luxury fashion companies to increase autonomy, authenticity and, consequently, consumer engagement.

In both luxury companies and their art foundations, the founder should be the fundamental pillar. They must project the values of their creators. Foundation managers should, therefore, invest resources toward maintaining the relevance and heritage of the brand to favor contamination of desired values that benefit both the foundation and the brand. The homonymy of the foundation and the luxury brand name should be preserved to maintain a "long-distance relationship" symbolized by the founder's name. However, the foundation and the brand should operate from separate headquarters to further enhance independence and prevent consumers from seeing the art foundation as a mere commercialization tool to improve the luxury brand's image or resonance. Failure to do this could neutralize the corporate benefits of the art foundation's values for the luxury company.

This case study is not exempt from limitations. In particular, in the Trussardi case, the synergic role of the founder preserves his heritage, as well as the contamination of corporate and foundation values, due to a homonymous family name. This is essential to maintaining the necessary connection for a profitable long-distance relationship between a luxury brand and its art foundation. Giving different names to the organizations, though stressing their autonomy, would relinquish this vital common heritage. Another limitation is the non-generalizability of the findings. The authors studied a single case to explore these dynamics, but other forms of art organizations in the luxury context could follow different relationship dynamics. Therefore, other luxury companies could consider the Trussardi case as more or less useful, according to their specific situations.

This study offers a new approach to identifying a profitable long-distance relationship between a luxury brand and its art foundation. Overcoming the traditional concept that art and luxury managers should integrate art and luxury in different ways to generate benefits for both parties, Trussardi offers a counterintuitive perspective in which the managed independence between the foundation and brand authentically enhance the founder's values. This suggests that consumers would better engage with both distinctive segments, while associating important values, such as rarity and universality, legitimization, tradition and innovation, with both the art foundation and the luxury company. These main findings open new perspectives on the role of corporate brand prominence in art exhibitions and other forms of art-luxury integration, which future studies could address. This study could, for example, be replicated in different international settings to understand how this art-luxury relationship may vary according to different cultural variables.

References

Carù, A., Ostillio, M. C., & Leone, G. (2017). Corporate museums to enhance brand authenticity in luxury goods companies: The case of Salvatore Ferragamo. *International Journal of Arts Management, 19*(2), 32–45.

Codignola, F., & Rancati, E. (2016). The blending of luxury fashion brands and contemporary art. In A. Vecchi & C. Buckley (Eds.), *Handbook of research on global fashion management and merchandising* (pp. 50–76). Hershey: IGI Global.

D'Arpizio, C., Levato, F., Prete, F., Del Fabbro, E., & de Montgolfier, J. (2019). *The future of luxury: A look into tomorrow to understand today.*

Retrieved February 6, 2020, from https://www.bain.com/insights/luxury-goods-worldwide-market-study-fall-winter-2018/ on March 9, 2019.

Fondazione Nicola Trussardi. (2020). The foundation. Retrieved March 6, 2020, from https://www.fondazionenicolatrussardi.com/en/the-foundation/.

Gregory, A. (2014, March 28). Art and fashion: The mutual appreciation society. *The Wall Street Journal.* Retrieved February 6, 2020, from http://www.wsj.com/articles/SB10001424052702303725404579459503054211692 on March 15, 2019.

Jackson, T., & Shaw, D. (2009). *Mastering fashion marketing.* Basingstoke, UK: Palgrave Macmillan.

Jelinek, J. S. (2018). Art as strategic branding tool for luxury fashion brands. *Journal of Product and Brand Management, 27*(3), 294–307.

Joy, A., Wang, J. J., Chan, T. S., Sherry, J. F., & Cui, G. (2014). M(Art)worlds: Consumer perceptions of how luxury brand stores become art institutions. *Journal of Retailing, 90*(3), 347–364.

Kapferer, J. N. (2012). Abundant rarity: The key to luxury growth. *Business Horizons, 55*(5), 453–462.

Kapferer, J. N. (2014). The artification of luxury: From artisans to artists. *Business Horizons, 57*(3), 371–380.

La Stampa. (2019, February 13). Trussardi: Storied fashion house acquired by asset management firm, QuattroR. *La Stampa.* Retrieved February 6, 2020, from https://www.lastampa.it/esteri/la-stampa-in-english/2019/02/13/news/trussardi-storied-fashion-house-acquired-by-asset-management-firm-quattror-1.33680815.

Nissley, N., & Casey, A. (2002). The politics of the exhibition: Viewing corporate museums through the paradigmatic lens of organizational memory. *British Journal of Management, 13*(S2), S35–S45.

Nobbs, K., Moore, C. M., & Sheridan, M. (2012). The flagship format within the luxury fashion market. *International Journal of Retail & Distribution Management, 40*(12), 920–934.

Okonkwo, U. (2007). *Luxury fashion branding: Trends, tactics, techniques.* Basingstoke, UK: Palgrave Macmillan.

Phau, I., & Prendergast, G. (2000). Consuming luxury brands: The relevance of the 'rarity principle'. *Journal of Brand Management, 8*(2), 122–138.

Pine, B., & Gilmore, J. (1999). *The experience economy.* Boston, MA: Harvard Business School Press.

Radón, A. (2012). Luxury brand exclusivity strategies: An illustration of a cultural collaboration. *Journal of Business Administration Research, 1*(1), 106.

Smith, M. O., Kubler, A., & Guinness, D. (2013). *Art/fashion in the 21st Century*. London, UK: Thames & Hudson.
Statista. (2019). *Trussardi: Turnover in 2011–2018.* Retrieved February 6, 2020, from https://www.statista.com/statistics/689620/turnover-of-italian-company-trussardi/.
Steele, V. (2012). Fashion. In A. Geczy & V. Karaminas (Eds.), *Fashion and art* (pp. 13–28). London, UK: Berg.
Teixeira, T. S., Wedel, M., & Pieters, R. (2010). Moment-to-moment optimal branding in TV commercials: Preventing avoidance by pulsing. *Marketing Science, 29*(5), 783–804.
Twist, K. V. (2005). Foreword. In C. Evans, S. Menkes, T. Polhemus, & B. Quinn (Eds.), *Hussein Chalayan.* Rotterdam, Netherlands: Nai Publishers.

4

Guccification: Redefining Luxury Through Art—The Gucci Revolution

Giorgia Sepe and Alessia Anzivino

Abstract This chapter focuses on Gucci, a successful luxury company that has managed to renew its brand and revolutionize its business model by employing artification strategies based on contamination. *Guccification* is a term first used by the company itself to its intent to make all its clothes and accessories express a Gucci style. Today, after the launch of this complex, visionary strategy, Guccification represents a successful marriage of fashion, art, and ethical issues driven by new leadership under chief executive officer (CEO) Marco Bizzarri and creative director Alessandro Michele. The chapter explores how Gucci is evolving into an art-oriented company due to the revolutionary vision of its creative leadership. Indeed, the brand is being transformed from a simple fashion

G. Sepe (✉) · A. Anzivino
Università Cattolica Del Sacro Cuore, Milan, Italy
e-mail: giorgia.sepe@unicatt.it

A. Anzivino
e-mail: alessia.anzivino@unicatt.it

M. Massi and A. Turrini (eds.), *The Artification of Luxury Fashion Brands*, Palgrave Studies in Practice: Global Fashion Brand Management,
https://doi.org/10.1007/978-3-030-26121-4_4

company into a cultural icon. Accordingly, its commitment to artification can be analyzed from three different perspectives: art within fashion, an artistic business vision, and a culture of purpose. This chapter examines how the Gucci brand has been able to redefine luxury by bringing together art and fashion, leading a new, emerging movement.

Keywords Artification · Art & Brand Contaminations · Fashion · Guccification · Kering · Luxury

Introduction

The relationship between art and luxury is not a simple coincidence (Chailan, 2018). Indeed, art arguably can enhance both the symbolic and the aesthetic aspects of brand perceptions and may help overcome the problems associated with the industrialization of luxury (Chailan, 2018; Kapferer, 2014; Lee, Chen, & Wang, 2015). Among the companies attempting to invest in their relationship with art, Gucci presents a focused, innovative example.

Gucci was founded in Florence in 1921 by Guccio Gucci, a small artisan specialized in leather articles, gloves, and suitcases. During the 1960s and 1970s, Gucci underwent a global expansion, becoming a symbol of industrial development while maintaining a strong commitment to artisanal production. Indeed, the Florentine headquarters continues to maintain strict control over product quality.

During the early 1990s, however, the fashion house faced a period of crisis. In a wide expansion, the Gucci brand produced a heterogeneous series of products, but consequently, it lost the specialization that made the company globally famous. This led to personnel changes, entrusting management of the label to Domenico De Sole and Tom Ford from 1994 to 2004. Ford, in particular, transformed the brand identity and gave the Italian fashion house a new style that established a formidable brand identity and strength. Ford was responsible for the design of all the product lines and the company's corporate image and advertising campaigns.

In 1999, Kering, a worldwide global luxury group founded by François-Henri Pinault, began to acquire shares of the Italian fashion brand. In 2004, Kering raised its stake in Gucci Group to 99.4%. Kering's vision of "embracing creativity for a modern, bold vision of luxury" drove a multi-brand business model based on the creative autonomy of its various houses. Throughout the 1990s, Gucci grew to become one of the most desirable Italian luxury fashion brands. After Ford left Gucci, Frida Giannini became creative director until 2015, when Bizzarri, the new president and CEO, chose her.

In 2015, the new era of Alessandro Michele began. As soon he obtained the role of creative director, Michele demonstrated his commitment by undertaking art exhibitions, supporting artists, and developing a role as a promoter of art and culture. For example, the Gucci Museum in Florence was renewed and renamed the Gucci Garden. The collection was presented through cultural and artistic fashion shows, many of which supported art exhibitions. Michele attempted to differentiate Gucci from its competitors, starting a revolution to transform Gucci from a fashion industry into a cultural industry firm. This initiative, named Guccification, made the fashion house into the most valuable Italian luxury brand in 2019, increasing its market share by 50% from 2018.

This case study shows how a company constituting a significant part of a global group has grown in a fragmented global luxury market characterized by a few large multi-brand groups and small independent players competing in different segments. In particular, Gucci's artistic directors have tried to bring together ethics and aesthetics and to use art to create exclusive experiences linked to the brand also drawing attention to the brand's heritage through contamination.

Following a brief overview of the history of the Gucci fashion house focused on the acquisition by the Kering Fashion Group to explain the company's background, this chapter examines Gucci's new creative leadership, highlighting its strong commitment to art. The analysis employed secondary data. In particular, data were gathered from a variety of documents including the company's annual and financial reports, the company's website and social media. We also looked at newspapers, trade and academic journals, books, articles, websites, and other media sources both in English and in Italian.

The chapter is structured as follows. The first section is dedicated to a company overview explaining the link between the Gucci brand and the concepts of contamination and artification. The second section provides details about Gucci's history, from its foundation to its acquisition by Kering, and shares Gucci's financial data. The third section analyzes Gucci as a creative industry firm, giving particular consideration to the artification process. The last section presents the discussion and conclusions of the case study, explaining why Gucci is an interesting example of artification in the fashion industry.

Company Overview

Before delving into the history of Gucci, it is important to explain the reasons why this company represents contamination based artification better than other brands. Artification can be seen as a consequence of the "general objectification of culture occurring in many societies" (Shapiro, 2004, p. 2), and along with the democratization of art, many contexts such as luxury fashion have adopted it. Among them, Gucci has been able to explore new ways of deploying art within fashion and to strengthen its reputation as a luxury brand by supporting it through a contamination experience.

Gucci is an Italian luxury fashion company founded in Florence in 1921 by Guccio Gucci, a small artisan employed in the luxury hotel sector in Paris and London. Moving to Florence, he founded the Guccio Gucci company as an artisanal firm specialized in leather articles, gloves, and suitcases. In the beginning, the company was named Gucci, and the first brand logo probably was derived from the founder's signature (Gucci, 2020a). Italian aristocrats were keen on horseracing in the 1930s, so Guccio Gucci tried to meet their needs by proposing a miniature horse-bit consisting of a double ring joined by a bar, with the green-red-green weft tape that incorporated a traditional saddle girth (Museo del Marchio Italiano, 2020). In 1955, the logo became a knight with a suitcase and a travel bag.

Distinctive to the brand, it became a ribbon inspired by a saddle girth and came in different sizes, in wool or cotton, and in green-red-green colors for articles in natural leather and in blue-red-blue for colored leathers. Over time, the logo changed and became more similar to the one used today. In the 1960s, the company decided to use a logo with the double "GG." Specifically, in 1960, Aldo Gucci, one of Guccio's sons, proposed the symbol of the two crossed "Gs," but only in 1992 did the symbol of the double "G" officially appear in the corporate brand.

Gucci's mission is to gain leadership in the world luxury market and to be perceived as a cool, responsible brand. Corporate social responsibility is a fundamental part of Gucci's global strategy, which is always based on the importance of craftsmanship. Gucci's mission also embraces willingness to use its leadership to pioneer and promote sustainability. Gucci's involvement in ethical matters began in 2004, with a study on sustainability strategies, which became part of its quality concept. Today, Gucci's target group includes the middle and upper classes, particularly people who invest in fashion, sustainability, and luxury.

Company History

After its founding in 1921, Gucci went through a number of evolutions. Gucci's worldwide expansion during the 1960s and 1970s gave the company an increasingly strong global presence, but its industrial development did not mean a revolution in its product schemes. They remained artisanal and managed and organized by the Florentine headquarters, which maintained strict control over product quality.

In the early 1990s, after a difficult financial period for the company, management was entrusted to De Sole, as president and CEO, and Ford, as creative director, who worked as a team at Gucci from 1994 to 2004. Particularly interesting were the contributions of Ford, who transformed the identity of the brand, and came up with a new style for the Florentine house, remixing classic and modern attributes, tradition, and innovation. He was also able to perceive the importance of advertising campaigns and started to collaborate with famous photographers such as Richard Avedon and Herb Ritts. Indeed, during Ford's time at Gucci, sales increased from $230 million in 1994 to almost $3 billion in 2003, making the company one of the most profitable luxury brands in the world (Tom Ford, 2020).

Table 4.1 Gucci's financial data

In € millions	2018	2017	Increase (%)
Revenue	8284.9	6211.2	+33.4
EBITDA	3514	2331.0	+50.8
Gross operating investments	312.7	248.5	+25.8

Source 2018 Financial document—Kering

After Ford left Gucci in 2002, Frida Giannini became creative director and relaunched the brand. Along with her future husband Patrizio di Marco as CEO, she continued the expansion process begun under Ford. After some years of great success, the company slowed down and went through a crisis toward the end of their management. Consequently, in 2015, Gucci was assigned a new president and CEO, Bizzarri, who came from successful experience with the group's Bottega Veneta, and a new creative director, Michele.

Bizzarri, as the new CEO, bet on Michele to relaunch the image and aesthetics of the brand. The pair started a new ambitious project, and Michele started to translate his colorful, romantic, poetic vision as a philosopher into a new strong positioning strategy for the whole brand. His efforts resulted in 33.4% sales growth from 2017 to 2018, with 8.3 billion euros in annual sales (Bowles, 2019). Table 4.1 compares the main financial data from 2017 and 2018 and shows the increase in both revenue and gross operating investment in one year.

Today, the brand markets modern items based on Bizzarri's approach continuously combining different styles and opposite universes such as the Italian Renaissance, Gothic aesthetics, and punk looks.

The Kering Acquisition

The Gucci Group is part of Kering's global luxury group, which manages the development of many renowned houses in fashion and luxury. Along with its competitors, LVMH (a French group held by Bernard Arnaud),

Hermès, Prada, Burberry, Chanel, and Richemont, Kering constitutes the most relevant group in the global personal luxury goods market.[1]

Kering was founded as Pinault Etablissements in Rennes, France, in 1963 by François Pinault and first specialized in timber trading. In 1987, the heir to the group, François-Henri Pinault, entered the company (which changed its name to PRR, Pinault Distribution) after graduating from HEC Business School in Paris. Soon, Pinault SA (PPR) entered the Paris Stock Exchange and started to rise. During the 1990s, it repositioned itself in the distribution sector, becoming one of the leading European groups in fashion luxury. Today, Kering ranks first on the Dow Jones Sustainability Index in the textiles, apparel, and luxury goods category, and it brings together a pool of trademarked brands including Gucci, Saint Laurent, Alexander McQueen, Bottega Veneta, Balenciaga, Brioni, Stella McCartney, Sergio Rossi, Boucheron, Dodo, Girard-Perregaux, Pomellato, and PUMA (Pavione, Pezzetti, & Matteo, 2016). Kering has 44,000 employees and sells more than $70 billion every year. In 2018, the group sold most of its PUMA shares, retaining only a minor 15.7% share, and it plans to sell off Volcom because its main aim is to focus only on luxury brands.

Pinault, the president and CEO, is an environmentalist and has worked to get Kering named as the top sustainable textile, apparel, and luxury goods corporation in the world. Indeed, he encourages all of the group's brands to pursue sustainable approaches by applying his slogan: "empowering imagination" (Pavione et al., 2016). Moreover, Pinault is considered to be an important supporter and promoter of art. As a patron, he has funded and followed many artistic projects over the years. For instance, in 2006, he contributed to the renovation of the Grand Canal building in Venice and the inauguration of Palazzo Grassi and Punta della Dogana, two museums restored by Japanese architect Tadao Ando. In 2014, Pinault promoted the creation of a common headquarters and artistic hub for Gucci in Milan. In 2019, following the tragic fire at Notre Dame in Paris, he pledged 101 million euros for its renewal and rebuilding and promised to devote resources and skills to the restoration

[1]According to Kering's (2018) financial report, the worldwide personal luxury goods market is divided into four main product categories: accessories, apparel, hard luxuries, and fragrances and cosmetics.

of the cathedral, a symbol of French identity (Friedman, 2019). Pinault's and Kering's vision of "embracing creativity for [a] modern, bold vision of luxury," is supported by a multi-brand business model that combines agility, balance, and responsibility and is based on the creative autonomy of the various houses and a clear strategy of letting the potential of luxury goods increase faster than the markets (Kering, 2020).

In 1999, Kering first acquired a controlling stake (42%) in Gucci as one of the key steps to create a coherent, complementary set of major luxury brands within the group. In 2004, Kering raised its stake in Gucci Group to 99.4% after a tender offer. Nevertheless, it is interesting to note that after the acquisition, the headquarters remained in Florence, with part of the management based in Milan. The main reason was to maintain the brand's Italian fashion tradition in the perceptions of final consumers around the world.

Figure 4.1 shows the simplified organizational distribution of brands within the group, divided into luxury, eyewear, and sports. As shown in Fig. 4.1, the group's strategy is mainly aimed at vertically integrating the brands by acquiring them to secure raw materials sourcing and logistic activities. Regarding the sports division, in April 2019, Kering announced the sale of its United States sports and lifestyle brand Volcom to Authentic Brands Group, which purchased the brand's intellectual property rights effective from April 1, 2019.

The year 2018 saw exceptional growth for Kering. These results were strongly impacted by the exceptional growth of the leading brand, Gucci (Fig. 4.2), which accounted for almost two-thirds of the consolidated revenue.

In 2017, Kering undertook a mission to carry out a strong digital transformation and take the lead in Customer Relationship Management, data science, and innovation because statistics show that e-commerce is the fastest-growing channel for all the group's luxury houses and accounted for 6% of its total retail sales in the first half of 2018 (Kering, 2018). As shown in Table 4.2, in 2018, Gucci continued its outstanding growth. Its performance has been well balanced among all its product categories and different targets.

Gucci's outstanding growth is based on the excellence of its business model and the continuous attention it gives to optimization of its

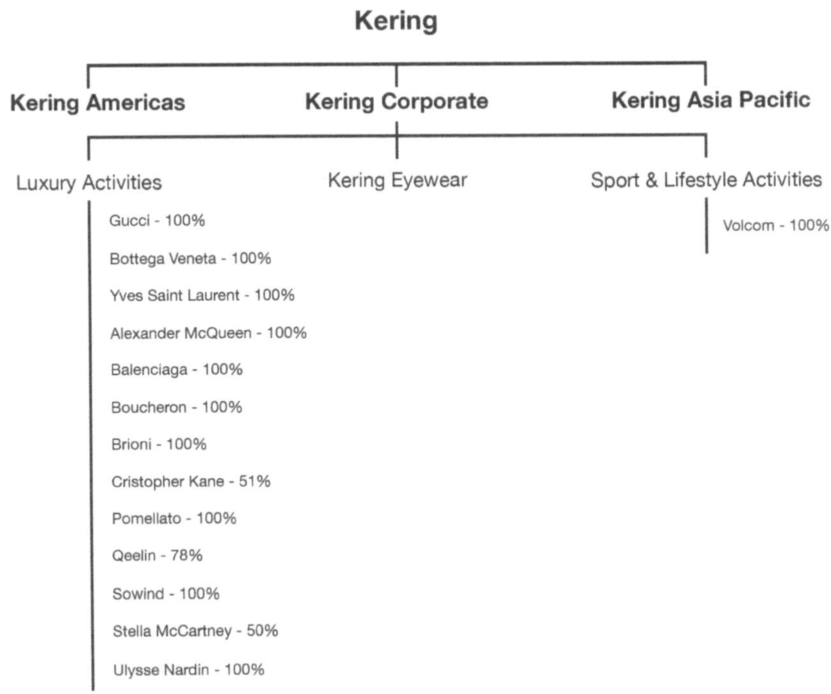

Fig. 4.1 Kering's portfolio of brands (*Source* Kering Financial Report—2018)

business model. All Gucci products reflect the new brand aesthetic and creative vision. Its product offerings have been optimized in terms of models and price clusters. During the past years, Gucci has worked on customer inclusivity, particularly in distribution policies. Furthermore, the new store concept has helped increase sales density.

Artification Strategy

Gucci has carried out an artification strategy since 2015, when the company appointed a new creative director (Alessandro Michele), a new president and CEO (Marco Bizzarri), and a new worldwide director of communications (Alessio Vannetti). It can be argued that with these appointments, the year 2015 sent a strong signal of a new era for the

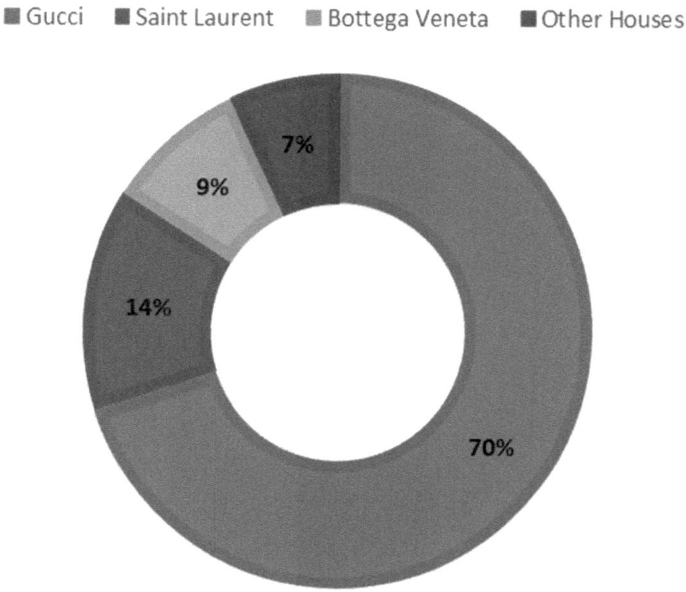

Fig. 4.2 Breakdown of revenue in 2018 by brand (*Source* Authors' elaboration based on 2018 Financial document—2018)

Table 4.2 Financial indicators—Kering

In € millions	2017	2018	%
Revenue	10,815.9	13,665.2	+26.3
Recurring operating income	2690.7	3943.8	+46.6
Net income, Group share	1785.6	3714.9	+108.1
Recurring net income, Group share (excluding non-recurring items)	1886.6	2816.7	+49.3

Source Authors' elaboration based on the 2018 Kering Financial Report

Italian company. Gucci has attempted to change the nature of its brand from exclusively retail and has transformed itself into part of the cultural industry.

In general, artification occurs in luxury fashion when arts and fashion present commonalities. For instance, luxury products made for cultural elites (Kapferer, 2014) present aesthetic features aimed at satisfying needs far from simply functional. Consequently, art and luxury are getting closer to the point that art has been defined as the cornerstone of luxury brands (Soito, 2018).

Michele, who was born in Rome in 1972, had been working for Gucci since 2002 when he was appointed senior designer of accessories under Ford's supervision. Michele has always been considered to be a philosopher designer because of his passion for mixing fashion, art, culture, and philosophy. In 2015, the new CEO and President Bizzarri decided to bet on the unknown, internal figure of Michele, to bring Gucci back and to try to change its positioning on the market.

Consequently, since 2015, Gucci has experimented with significant changes in many ways from a cultural perspective. Instead of focusing on simply commercializing fashion products, the firm has shifted its overall strategy to invert the cultural paradigm by integrating an aesthetic and a wider culture that exceeds being a mere luxury fashion brand and capitalizes on this by distributing commercial products. This has redefined luxury through an artistic and cultural paradigm and consequently has branded art through fashion and luxury. This new strategy completely aligned with Michele's vision is represented by the renewed Gucci Museum in Florence, revolutionized fashion collections, and ancillary projects between the brand and the art institutions, including shows and exhibitions. As Vanessa Friedman[2] (2018) wrote in a *New York Times* review after one of Michele's first shows, he is more than a creative director and a fashion diplomat; he is also a cultural leader. She calls the fashion house "the United Nation of Gucci" because it unites the world with the language of clothes. Gucci thus is moving toward being a creative industry firm in which the dimensions of digital communication and editorial thought walk together. The Gucci Garden, a historical museum, represents the most important interface between Gucci and its public and produces a new system of meanings through actors' interactions with all of its collections and objects.

Gucci's commitment to art, following the overall mindset of its patron Pinault, has become even stronger thanks to the revolutionary vision of

[2]Vanessa Friedman has been the fashion director and chief fashion critic for *The New York Times* since March 2014.

its new creative leader. The brand has evolved from a simple fashion company into a cultural icon involved in promoting art, culture, and values of gender equality and addressing new, challenging topics. Today, Gucci's mission is "to bring positive change in order to secure a collective future" (Equilibrium Gucci, 2020). This corporate strategy has yielded fruits in brand value and perceptions. In the BrandZ Top 30 Most Valuable Italian Brands 2019, Gucci ranks first among the 30 Italian luxury brands in the world. As the report states, "Gucci stands strong as Italy's most valuable brand after growing 50%, in a ranking flush with luxury brands" (Millwardbrown, 2020).

Gucci's overall strategy and commitment to art can be analyzed from three perspectives. As depicted in Fig. 4.3, Gucci incorporates art within fashion through contamination, development of a visible artistic vision, and implementation of a culture of purpose. These three categories contribute to positioning Gucci as one of the strongest creative industry firms within the fashion and luxury segment.

The following sections investigate these three perspectives in depth to explain how Gucci has joined the creative industry and made a strong commitment to art in all of its divisions.

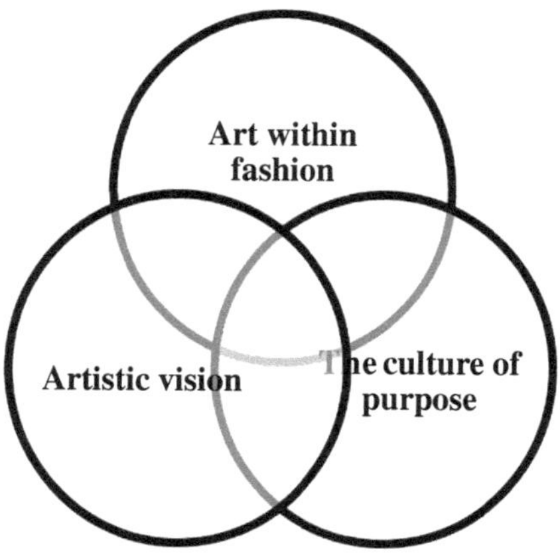

Fig. 4.3 Gucci's commitment to art (*Source* Authors' elaboration)

Art Within Fashion

Gucci's vision of the role of art in fashion includes all the strategies the company has developed and implemented in recent years. Since his arrival, Michele has completely revolutionized Gucci's fashion collection and creations, making art a strong dimension in all his propositions. As Vannetti (2019) stated during a national conference on fashion and luxury held in Milan, "one of the first things you are taught when you become director of communications is that you have to never speak about sex, religion, and politics. Then I saw the first show made by Michele, and everything was put together. The beauty of the creativity that comes from Alessandro and the team is that everything goes on at the same time." The following timeline (Fig. 4.4) shows the most significant events from 2015 to 2019 that deal with fashion and art and have positioned Gucci as the protagonist of significant changes.

In 2016, Gucci launched a new project: Gucci 4 Rooms. For this project, four artists were asked to create a room inspired by the themes and motives introduced by Michele. This was among the first of the company's innovative projects in which art and fashion contaminate each other, as do the online and the offline, the digital and the analogical. Based on contamination between art and fashion, the rooms included the following: the Gucci Herbarium Room by Chiharu Shiota, the Gucci Garden Room, populated by animals and vegetation of the Maison's iconographic garden; the Gucci Words Room, by Daito Manabe and the last, by Trouble Andrew, who created a secret art installation.

In line with previous events and strategies, in 2017, Michele proposed the Guccification Cruise Collection, mixing Renaissance and pop art and recognizing the value of Italian culture and the Florentine tradition. This

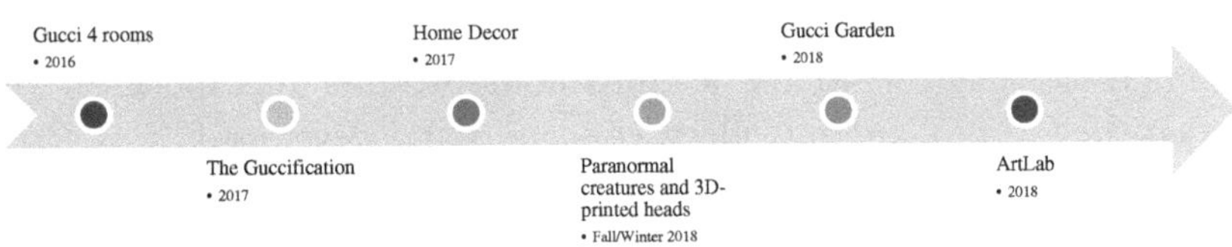

Fig. 4.4 Art within fashion: A timeline of events from 2015 to 2019 (*Source* Authors' elaboration)

collection embodied the roots of Italian culture but was inspired by a pop and punk style.

Another important event took place during the presentation show of Gucci's fall/winter collection of 2018. In an aseptic scene, Makinarium, an Italian creative agency that does special effects for the cinema, contributed to the visual and special effects of dragons and chameleons. During the show, some models carried in their arms artisanal and 3D print reproductions of their own heads, as well as dragons and chameleons. These heads and dragons were single pieces of handmade artisanal products realized by Makinarium.

In 2017, Gucci launched Gucci Home Decor to celebrate artisanal knowledge and the success of Michele's collections. The same stylistic elements seen on the catwalk were shifted to the home and furnishing accessories, including a table set of plates, cups, and bowls with botanical prints. In this era of customization, Gucci Décor includes a rich collection of precious embroideries (with an ironic note that plays down everything), geometric patterns, designs recovered from the immense Gucci archive, and delicate floral shapes imprinted on furniture, furnishings, and tableware. Gucci uses Italian craftsmanship excellence to realize each product, from Richard Ginori's porcelain vases to Tuscan master artisans' velvet and leather chairs requiring 64 hours of manual work each (official website, 2019).

In addition, Gucci recently renewed its historical museum in Florence, transforming the Palazzo della Mercanzia building into a fashion garden called the Gucci Garden. The building is split into three different spaces through which storytelling drives customers and visitors. On the ground floor, there is a boutique to buy unique goods and limited-edition goods created only for the Gucci Garden. Another space is devoted to the Osteria di Massimo Bottura, a three-Michelin-star restaurant, because the culture of recycling food and avoiding food wasting is relevant to the company's strategic vision. The third floor presents an exposition area named the Gucci Garden Gallery, conceived and developed by art critic Maria Luisa Frisa and incorporating the company's artistic and strategic vision.

Finally, Gucci created ArtLab, a futuristic center of industrial craftsmanship and experimental laboratory in the historical headquarters of the fashion house near Florence. This laboratory was inaugurated personally by Pinault and Bizzarri. In this center, the fashion house can prototype and sample leather goods and shoes. According to Bizzarri, Gucci ArtLab "is the perfect expression of the corporate culture that we have been building and nurturing within the company. It is the tangible expression of a place to learn skills and techniques, a workshop to generate ideas, and ideas are the lifeblood of culture." Inside the ArtLab, the Ècole de l'Amour was opened in October 2018 to offer an education program designed to train new craftsmen. There are multiple schools. The first is Craftsmanship School that is a six-month program with the aim to educate trainees in the product design and production process of leather goods. The Factory School (Scuola di Fabbrica) is a two-month program to train production operators specialized in the specific manufacturing operations of leather goods. Finally, the Technical Academy can train employees working in different departments.

Artistic Vision

The second category is an artistic vision. Gucci has clearly embedded art within its strategic vision. According to the company, developing an artistic vision means 360-degree involvement in art by participating in exhibitions and celebrating artists. The company has developed various initiatives to strengthen its artistic identity and its willingness to be relevant to the world of art, contributing in original ways.

Figure 4.5 illustrates the most significant initiatives conceived and implemented by the company. In particular, Gucci has carried out four

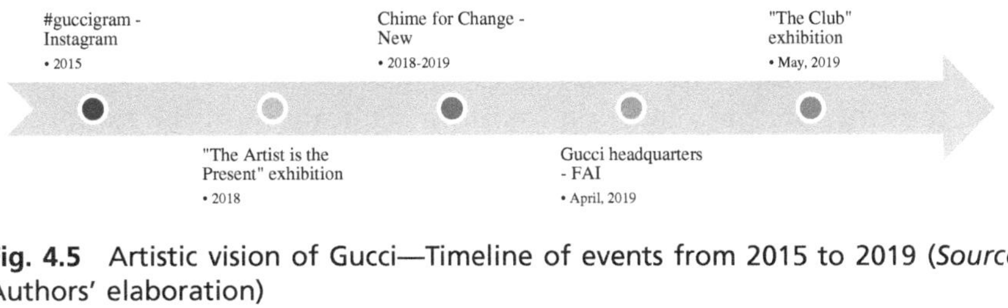

Fig. 4.5 Artistic vision of Gucci—Timeline of events from 2015 to 2019 (*Source* Authors' elaboration)

different initiatives under Michele's supervision: "The Artist is the Present"; a new chapter of the Chime for Change project; the opening of the Fondo Ambiente Italiano (FAI) headquarters in Milan during the Italian culture days; and, most recently, "The Club" exhibition. Soon after his arrival in 2015, Michele launched the Guccigram project on Instagram (#guccigram). For this promotional initiative, the creative director invited some emerging artists to create artworks paired with Gucci products. This project was closely linked to another successful initiative in 2018 developed with the Italian famous artist Maurizio Cattelan.

In October 2018, Gucci launched a new project for an exhibition featuring Cattelan in the Yuz Museum of Shanghai. The exhibition entitled "The Artist is Present" dealt with the age of copying and revealed the excellence of China, which unfortunately is mostly known as a country of forgeries and replications. In a deliberate provocation, the name was taken from Marina Abramovic's show "The Artist is Present" (which took place in the MoMa Museum of New York in 2010) and was used to promote ArtWalls in Shanghai. The exhibition was aimed at exploring how replicating art can still make original art and how originals can be preserved through copies. Physics confirms that in nature, "nothing is created, nothing is destroyed, everything is transformed," so Cattelan wanted to demonstrate that this principle can easily be transferred to art and reworking art. He selected artworks by more than thirty artists from China and throughout the world to participate in the exhibition. Michele also wanted to celebrate fake replications of the brand Gucci, stating that even replications express a form of love for a brand.

As Vannetti stated, the project generated business results but also demonstrated a strong commitment to a country where the Gucci language spoke of both perfection and replication as two different but complementary values. Due to the unexpected success of the exhibition, the Chinese government rewarded and recognized Gucci's inimitable value, and countries around the world asked for replications of the exhibition, which Michele and Cattelan both refused to do. Although the idea of not being able to replicate an exhibition based on replication seemed oxymoronic, Maurizio Cattelan stated that Shanghai was the environment and an essential part of the exhibition.

In 2013, Gucci launched the global Chime for Change campaign closely related to Kering's vision. Through this campaign, it has funded more than 430 projects over the years and has supported values such as empowerment and inclusion. Promoters of this initiative are Salma Hayek Pinault and Beyoncé Knowles-Carter, and financial support comes from the Kering Foundation, Hearst Magazines, Facebook, and the Bill & Melinda Gates Foundation. Since 2013, this global campaign has raised more than $15 million to support projects around the world. As Gucci states in its official documents, "We believe that connection empowers us. That every voice matters. That each one of us is needed to achieve change. We believe we can do extraordinary things when we gather together. Explore the stories of changemakers around the world and the projects we support to help raise the next generation of leaders in the fight for gender equality."

In 2019, under the supervision of Michele, Gucci launched a new chapter of the Chime for Change campaign devoted to ArtWalls and creative collaborations aimed at strengthening its commitment to a more equitable world through the support of art. As stated by Michele, "Every person is created equal. We all have the power to use our voices to stand up for what we believe in." Indeed, the campaign is devoted to harnessing the power of a new generation to promote gender equality, global employee engagement, and women's empowerment. In the cities of London, Milan, New York, Taiwan, and Hong Kong, Gucci has exploited its ArtWalls to picture unidentifiable human figures standing together. The work was made by Italian visual artist MP5, who applied her black-and-white style in making the figures. In her biography, the Italian female artist, muralist, and illustrator presents her techniques and mediums for drawing on newspapers, magazines, and video and audio animations (MP5, 2020)

More recently, during the Italian FAI Spring Days in March 2019,[3] Gucci first opened up its new headquarters in Milan for the public to visit. As stated by Bizzarri on the company's official website, the place has been transformed "from an old industrial area [and] hosts an open and

[3]FAI is an Italian non-profit founded in 1975 with the aim to protect and enhance Italy's historical, artistic, and landscape heritage. Every year, during the Spring Days, it opens some historical places to visitors.

modern work environment at the base of the concept of learning organization." The aim of this initiative was to become the new headquarters part of Italian artistic heritage during one of the most important days for the preservation of history and art.

The most recent initiative between the Gucci house and an artist was Emiliano Maggi's artistic exhibition at the Nomas Foundation in Rome, Italy (Inside Art, 2019). The aim of the exhibition, as stated by the artist, was to "communicate certain freedom to be, and wear, what [everybody] wants" (Gucci, 2020b). The exhibition was supported by Gucci's aesthetic vocabulary, using clothes as a living material in artistic sculptures.

Art, culture, and fashion also drove Gucci's most recent collection, Cruise 2020. Inspired by the works at Capitoline Museum, Michele presented a collection in which Roman tunics, peplums, and togas stood out and were mixed with references to the contemporary world. He tried to connect to the classical era and paganism of Ancient Rome, representing an aesthetic imaginary and a moment of freedom.

A Culture of Purpose

The third category is the so-called culture of purpose, which is rooted in the general idea that the company does everything for a reason. Based on the culture of purpose philosophy, artification finds its own *raison d'être.*

Culture of purpose relates to the value of integrity, as it is aimed at managing and respecting the limited resources that come from the planet. The culture of purpose encompasses the new decennial sustainability plan for the brand Gucci launched in 2017. As confirmed by *The New York Times* (O'Grady, 2019), Michele's whole strategy is based on "A Cyborg Manifesto," in which Haraway (1994) explains feminism and socialism during the 1980s. "A Cyborg Manifesto" inspired Michele's whole revolutionizing strategy as the company's creative director because Haraway's cyborgs represent a set of ideals of a race-less, genderless, and more peaceful civilization.

This new idea of a culture of purpose emerged during the development of the project called Equilibrium, which includes all of the brand's values, positive instincts, and ambitions. Equilibrium means balancing the aesthetic and the ethical elements. Based on the culture of purpose, Gucci's artification is based on a balance among the environment (the laurel crown), people, and new models (the balance). The first element of Equilibrium is the environment, which involves protecting the earth and advancing sustainability to become a real agent of change. The second element of people represents Gucci's aim to encourage diversity and gender equality, which requires empowering employees within both the company and the supply chain. Indeed, as stated on the company's website, Gucci has been recognized as a "top employer" in Italy for creating a commission to build new welfare plan to help employees balance their work and life.

The third element of new models refers to the aim to change production processes, raw materials, and approaches and make them more sustainable. Gucci's new models also includes the innovative ArtLab project founded in 2018, already mentioned before.

Another new model initiative is Gucci Changemakers, which aims to empower employees worldwide to dedicate 1% of their working time to volunteer with preferred non-profit organizations involved in gender equality, refugee, homeless, education, and environmental causes. The initiative was launched internally in 2018, and its most ambitious goal is to create a major turning point in the fashion world, strengthening its social impacts and relationships with local communities. Attention to the environment, people, and production process—these are the three pillars in which Gucci is investing to give concrete expression to its concept of sustainability.

Everything Gucci does is for a certain reason and also artification and contamination between art and fashion have to be considered as a consequence of the culture of purpose.

Conclusion and Implications

This chapter has dealt with the Gucci case as an instance of artification based on contamination. Contaminations, as stated in Chapter 1, are collaborations between art and luxury that create a sort of infusion effect, and Gucci is a good example of this type of artification. In particular, contamination in Gucci emerges from the brand's personality and has been so successful over the years that in the 1990s, fashion insiders came up with a new expression: "doing a Gucci" (Heller, 2000). This phrase refers to Gucci's transformation in the mid-1990s from near bankruptcy (with losses in the tens of millions of dollars) into, first, the target of a highly contested takeover and, then, a global powerhouse. The contributions of De Sole and Ford made Gucci into the world's third most valuable fashion brand with a value of more than $8.76 billion in 2011.

Then, in 2015, Michele began a new profitable era for the company, considerably changing the brand value and positioning and starting what we have called the "Guccification" movement. Indeed, as discussed in this chapter, Gucci's vision and strategy moved it into first place in the Top 30 Most Valuable Italian Brands of 2019, after growing 50%, in a ranking flush with luxury brands.

Today, Gucci is shifting to become a creative industry firm in which the dimensions of digital communication and editorial thought walk together. The company's commitment to art, following the overall mindset of its patron Pinault, president of Kering, has become even stronger due to the revolutionary vision of its creative leadership. Its mission is "to bring positive change in order to secure a collective future" in three areas: fashion within art, artistic vision, and a culture of purpose (Icon, 2020).

The effort to pair luxury products and art, and the tension to the contamination between art and fashion, represent a marketing strategy to increase perceptions of products as luxurious (Huettl & Gierl, 2012; Peluso, Pino, Amatulli, & Guido, 2017). Gucci's new positioning is continuously improving consumers' evaluations and intentions to buy its various products (Huettl & Gierl, 2012; Lee et al., 2015; Peluso et al., 2017). Differentiating products based on their functional features and attributes has become difficult, so the symbolic meanings of products have become fundamental (Govers & Schoormans, 2005), especially if they are committed to art, in a logic of creation of mutual benefits for art and fashion.

Thus, Gucci's introduction of the art theme seems to be a systematic strategy, not a coincidence, as confirmed by the study of Chailan (2018), who stated that the relationships between the art world and luxury brands are systematic and not due to simple coincidence. Art enhances the symbolic and aesthetic value of brand perceptions and usually overcomes problems related to the industrialization of luxury (Chailan, 2018; Kapferer, 2014; Lee et al., 2015). Art introduction is a strategy to give value to the past and to add contents to begin new stories closely linked to the past. It is important to emphasize that today, art has the task to create new and different worlds that defend the brand's "made in Italy" and, at the same time, reach new audiences (Fulco, 2019). Consequently, the new art-based brand Gucci seems to be an activator of collaboration between artists and exclusive products and services while giving importance to continuous alignment with its target consumers (Fulco, 2019). This case study supports that art is also central in the strategies of luxury brands because it is able to constantly renew itself and elevate a luxury brand from the ordinary to the extraordinary. Moreover, one critical success factor seems to be building strong collaborations with artists based on trust, not only commercial objectives.

The process of Guccification introduced by Michele and his revolutionary vision cannot be easily replicated by other luxury brands, confirming what the literature reports about art-related strategies: competitors have difficulty replicating a judicious art-related strategy, for example, because of the competencies needed to excel (Chailan, 2018). Moreover, Gucci's strong commitment to ethical causes such as gender equality, feminism, and environmentalism make it a pioneer of the 360-degree marriage of fashion, art, and attention to ethical issues.

Art has been useful for Gucci to enhance its exclusivity and uniqueness, emphasize its characteristics, and distance itself from the nonluxury world by raising the entry barriers for all other luxury brands that try to imitate or reach it. Art has been also useful for Gucci to improve its market penetration and to transfer positive associations to consumers (Lee et al., 2015; Masè, Cedrola, & Cohen-Cheminet, 2018). Partnerships with artists are also useful for this luxury brand to attract brand non-core customers, because their personalities are more drawn to the artists than the brand itself. This type of alliance does not damage Gucci's customers who already appreciate the brand (Kim, Chang, Vaidyanathan, & Stoel, 2018). This case clearly shows how contamination continuously influences consumer evaluation of the brand and how the brand has benefited from the use of art, leading to mutual benefits for both art and fashion.

References

Bowles. (2019). *Inside the wild world of Gucci's Alessandro Michele.* Retrieved March 3, 2020, from https://www.vogue.com/article/gucci-alessandro-michele-interview-may-2019-issue.

Chailan, C. (2018). Art as a means to recreate luxury brands' rarity and value. *Journal of Business Research, 85,* 414–423.

Equilibrium Gucci. (2020). *CEO Carbon Neutral Challenge.* Retrieved March 3, 2020, from http://equilibrium.gucci.com/.

Friedman, V. (2018). The United Nation of Gucci, and Liberation by Dior. *New York Times.* Retrieved April 26, 2020, from https://www.nytimes.com/2018/09/25/fashion/gucci-dior-paris-fashion-week.html.

Friedman, V. (2019). French Titans' Pledges to Notre-Dame Pass €850 Million. *New York Times.* Retrieved March 3, 2020, from https://www.nytimes.com/2019/04/16/fashion/Donations-notre-dame-fire.html.

Fulco, E. (2019). L'impresa storica come fabbrica di cultura: tra Heritage e contaminazioni. *Economia della Cultura, 29*(1), 15–28.

Govers, P. C., & Schoormans, J. P. (2005). Product personality and its influence on consumer preference. *Journal of Consumer Marketing, 22*(4), 189–197.

Gucci. (2020a). *Il Gucci Garden.* Retrieved March 3, 2020, from https://www.gucci.com/it/it/st/stories/inspirations-and-codes/article/gucci_garden.

Gucci. (2020b). *The Club.* Retrieved March 3, 2020, from https://www.gucci.com/it/en_gb/st/stories/people-events/article/emiliano-maggi-exhibition-the-club.

Haraway, D. (1994). A manifesto for cyborgs: Science, technology, and socialist feminism in the 1980s. In S. Seidman (Ed.), *The postmodern turn: New perspectives on social theory* (pp. 82–115). Cambridge: Cambridge University Press.

Heller, R. (2000). Le brand, c'est moi. *Forbes Global, 13,* 74–83.

Huettl, V., & Gierl, H. (2012). Visual art in advertising: The effects of utilitarian vs hedonic product positioning and price information. *Marketing Letters, 23*(3), 893–904.

Icon. (2020). *Gucci launches equilibrium in a world-wide effort for sustainability.* Retrieved March 3, 2020, from https://icon.ink/articles/gucci-equilibrium-sustainability/.

Inside Art. (2019). *Le opere di Maggi in Dialogo con Gucci.* Retrieved March 3, 2020, from https://insideart.eu/2019/05/13/le-opere-di-maggi-con-i-tessuti-gucci/.

Kapferer, J. N. (2014). The artification of luxury: From artisans to artists. *Business Horizons, 57*(3), 371–380.

Kering. (2018). *Financial document.* Retrieved March 3, from https://keringcorporate.dam.kering.com/m/3ba17a6b64aae82d/original/2018-Financial-document.pdf.

Kering. (2020). *Our strategy.* Retrieved March 3, 2020, from https://www.kering.com/en/group/discover-kering/our-strategy/.

Kim, P., Chang, H., Vaidyanathan, R., & Stoel, L. (2018). Artist-brand alliances to target new consumers: Can visual artists recruit new consumers to a brand? *Journal of Product & Brand Management, 27*(3), 308–319.

Lee, H. C., Chen, W. W., & Wang, C. W. (2015). The role of visual art in enhancing perceived prestige of luxury brands. *Marketing Letters, 26*(4), 593–606.

Masè, S., Cedrola, E., & Cohen-Cheminet, G. (2018). Is artification perceived by consumers of luxury products? The research relevance of a customer-based brand equity model. *Journal of Global Fashion Marketing, 9*(3), 223–236.

Millwardbrown. (2020). *BrandZ Top Italian Brands.* Retrieved March 3, 2020, from http://www.millwardbrown.com/brandz/rankings-and-reports/top-italian-brands/2019.

MP5. (2020). *MP5.* Retrieved March 3, 2020, from http://www.mpcinque.com/mp5/.

O'Grady, M. (2019). *Fashions for the future.* Retrieved March 3, 2020 from https://www.nytimes.com/interactive/2019/03/21/t-magazine/fashion-future-history.html.

Pavione, E., Pezzetti, R., & Matteo, D. A. (2016). Emerging competitive strategies in the global luxury industry in the perspective of sustainable development: The case of Kering Group. *Management Dynamics in the Knowledge Economy, 4*(2), 241–261.

Peluso, A. M., Pino, G., Amatulli, C., & Guido, G. (2017). Luxury advertising and recognizable artworks: New insights on the "art infusion" effect. *European Journal of Marketing, 51*(11/12), 2192–2206.

Shapiro R. (2004). Qu'est-ce que l'artification? *Actes du XVIIe Congrès de l'Association internationale de sociologie de langue française*. Tours.
Soito, P. (2018). Why art is the cornerstone of luxury brands. *Art Market Magazine*, 37.
Tom Ford. (2020). *About tom Ford*. Retrieved March 3, 2020, from https://www.tomford.com/about.
Vannetti, A. (2019, March 13). *Fashion Today: Gucci e la nuova comunicazione*. Conference held at Università Cattolica del Sacro Cuore, Milan.

5

Christian Dior: The Art of Haute Couture

Federica Antonaglia and Juliette Passebois Ducros

Abstract This chapter deals with Christian Dior, one of the leading brands in the contemporary luxury fashion sector. This chapter shows how artification operates in the Dior Couture fashion house, emerging as a form of hybridization between the brand and art. This chapter depicts the hybridization process, in the context of *Maison Dior*. It charts a process that emerges through three kinds of mechanisms. First, Dior celebrates its creator as an artist: the chapter shows how the Dior brand has been historically and genuinely linked to the world of art and how this is promoted today. Second, artification emerges through a heritagization process that drives consumers to consider Christian Dior as part of the French heritage and a key component of the French fashion history. Finally, the spectacularization of the fashion house cultivates a contemporary vision of the brand based on the creative director's work. Creative directors, have played a key role in making the brand appealing and avoiding the risk of "museification" or commoditization.

F. Antonaglia (✉) · J. Passebois Ducros
IAE—Enseignant Chercheur, University of Bordeaux, Bordeaux, France
e-mail: federica.antonaglia@u-bordeaux.fr

M. Massi and A. Turrini (eds.), *The Artification of Luxury Fashion Brands*,
Palgrave Studies in Practice: Global Fashion Brand Management,
https://doi.org/10.1007/978-3-030-26121-4_5

Keywords Artification · Dior · Haute couture · Art & brand hybridizations · Heritagization · Spectacularization

Introduction

Created in 1947 by the homonymous fashion designer, Christian Dior Fashion House (CD hereafter) is one of the most famous French fashion houses and one of the biggest brands in the LVMH luxury group, the world's leading luxury goods group (with revenue of $23.4MM in 2018). During the 1950s, after years of serious and strict wartime clothes, Christian Dior was able to impose his own new fashion style, known as the "New Look" (i.e., colorful, romantic, and feminine dresses). He also laid the foundations for a global luxury brand that is still attractive seventy years since its creation. The brand has risen to the challenges in the turbulent luxury market, successfully overcoming them.

Right from the beginning of the adventure, CD supported artists, was inspired by artistic movements, and maintained a strong relationship with artists and the art world. This aspect of the founder's life is today used by the brand to celebrate the creator as an artist and to underscore the fact that artistic links have always defined the CD identity. More recently, artification has taken the brand to the highest level of the artification process (Shapiro, 2004; Shapiro & Heinich, 2012, 2015), i.e., hybridization (see Chapter 1). Hybridization refers to an extreme level of interaction between high culture and commercial culture that generates "grafts" or new forms and genres. In this chapter, we have a twofold objective, that is: a) to analyze how the artification process took place in CD case and, b) to understand the mechanisms through which hybridization has emerged over time in this luxury house. To these ends, we have undertaken a two-step methodology. First, based on a literature review, we have established a former theoretical gird positing the main issues of artification and its different forms (i.e., synergies, contamination, hybridization). Secondly, we've gathered a large secondary data material based on interviews, official reports of Dior, books published on Christian Dior history, press articles, communication campaigns, blogs and so on (from 1956 to now, see Annex 1 for sources). This material has been analyzed through the theoretical gird that emerged from the literature review.

The data analysis drives to highlight two underlying and complementary stages of the hybridization process in CD case, namely, the heritagization (Davallon, 2006) and the spectacularization of the brand.

Heritagization, which Davallon (2006) defines as the process of acquiring the symbolic status of "something to be kept in contrast to the status of something that can be exchanged" (p. 2), is referring to actions prompted by LVMH group—which today owns the CD brand—to highlight the link to the artworld in a more explicit way in order to build the "brand heritage." It would be illustrated by the exhibitions dedicated to the brand, where great emphasis is placed on the friendship between Christian Dior and renowned artists such as Dalí. The highly artistic nature of the fashion designers who followed Christian Dior in guiding the creative direction of the fashion house is another example of heritagization. LVMH group strategically used the friendships and relationships between CD and artists over time in order to accentuate the brand's uniqueness. In the case of CD, heritagization occurs by developing a unique collection of CD's fashion creations (e.g., a heritage department has been created for this purpose at CD), with the conservation of the founder's personal creations that are preciously preserved and exhibited in permanent museums (e.g., the *Musée Christian Dior*) as well as in temporary exhibitions (the V&A in London, MAD decorative art museum in Paris, etc.). Heritagization, consequently, makes the brand timeless.

Concerning the second element of hybridization, i.e., spectacularization, the term refers to the modernization of the brand, needed to avoid the pitfalls of museification and to support the brand's future development (Dion & Arnould, 2011). In the CD case study, this spectacularization involves artistic directors who play a major role in the brand "performance." Specifically, we show how creative directors become brand artists, transforming the CD products into works of art. As artists, the presentations of their collections are considered as "happenings." Dior's top designers such as Galliano, Hedi Slimane, Raf Simons, and Maria Grazia Chiuri are closely linked to the contemporary artworld and the artistic community. This link is strategically developed by the brand to blur the lines between creative directors and artists.

Our chapter is organized as follows: (a) A Company Overview section gives to readers an idea of the strategy and of the financial performance of the brand, today owned by LVMH, the world's largest luxury group. Then (b) a company history section summarizes the beginning of the illustrious fashion house, followed by (c) the main paragraph dedicated to artification strategy. Here the celebration of the creator, the heritagization and the spectacularization of the brand are discussed as the forms in which hybridization of arts and culture happens within CD case. Finally (e) a discussion and implications final section concludes the chapter.

Company Overview

Christian Dior enjoys excellent financial performance overall, and benefits from a solid reputation worldwide. Based on the Best Global brand ranking, the CD brand value was estimated at $M5.3 (the brand ranks 91st), a value that recently increased by 15% (2017/2018, www.interbrand.com). While CD is a French brand, it is nonetheless active across the globe, with 198 retail stores worldwide. 76% of CD's sales are generated by exports (Michaud & Masure, 2018), with a predominant presence primarily in Asia, Europe, the US, and Japan. The US represents almost 25% of total revenue, while Europe (excluding France) accounts for 18% of total turnover (MarketLine, 2017). Today, the Asia-Pacific area is one of CD's main markets. This is not surprising given that, currently, 32% of luxury goods purchases are made by Chinese consumers (MarketLine, 2017). CD's success in foreign markets should not, however, make us forget that the market in which the brand operates is highly competitive as CD competes with several other iconic luxury brands, including Louis Vuitton, Prada, Hermes, Chanel, and Gucci among others.

One of CD's key success factors in the luxury market is its brand equity. The brand DNA is closely associated with the history of its creator and its glamorous "spirit." The CD brand does not exist in itself but draws its identity from its creator. CD is closely associated with "*elegant lines, femininity, beauty, timeless and inimitable attitude*" (LVMH.com). Supported by artistic directors, *Haute Couture* creations are a core aspect of the brand equity. Each creative director signs his/her own collection and gives the brand its unique value. This uniqueness is transmitted through fashion shows, as in the recent *Cruise show.*

Currently, the brand is present at three levels of luxury brand classification: *Griffe* (or absolute luxury), *Luxury brand*, and *Premium brand* (Kapferer, 2008; Kapferer & Bastien, 2012). Christian Dior is a *Griffe* (an iconic brand name) known as "Christian Dior Couture" for which the company produces unique and pure creations at the rate of two collections a year. Christian Dior Couture products target a relatively narrow market segment: from 200 to 300 customers in the world. Collections are produced under the patronage of a creative director. Since the death of Christian Dior, Yves Saint Laurent, John Galliano and, more recently, Maria Grazia Chiuri, have reinterpreted the Christian Dior spirit and signed the CD collections. Collections are made in eight workshops located in France and Italy.

Christian Dior is also a luxury brand with a ready-to-wear product line. This activity is marked by high quality, high price, scarcity, and aesthetic uniqueness. In this market segment, Christian Dior manufactures and sell's clothes, handbags, leatherwork, and accessories. The leatherwork items form a significant part of the activity, driven by iconic pieces such as the famous *Lady Dior* handbag. Endorsed by Princess Diana, this handbag has been highly successful (100,000 handbags were sold in the first year) and is still very popular with fashion addicts today. International stars, including Marion Cotillard, Jennifer Lawrence, and Rihanna, have endorsed Dior's brand image.

Finally, Christian Dior is also positioned as a premium brand through its perfumes and make-up products. Here, the brand markets reproducible and manufactured goods. *Miss Dior* (created in 1947) and the more recent *J'adore* and *Sauvage* are iconic products that Christian Dior himself launched and that represent a core activity for the brand, driving profitability in this segment. As Claude Martinez explained in an interview released in *Le figaro Economique* en 2004 to Sonia Devilliers "the great statutory perfumes are an element more indispensable than ever: launched on a world scale, they are the flagships of the brand far beyond the field of perfumes." The success of CD cosmetics and perfumes lies in its huge investment in research and development (1.2% of sales are dedicated to innovation) and the "muses" that endorse the brand in ads (e.g., Charlize Theron, Nathalie Portman, Robert Pattison, Mila Kunis, and Camille Rowe) (LVMH.com).

Hence, CD has maintained its tradition as a creator of recognized *Haute Couture* and, at the same time, has penetrated the global market, increasing its sales and revenue. This is a common business model for luxury brands belonging to large international groups (e.g., LVMH, Kering, etc.). The *Haute Couture* division promotes the prestigious reputation of the global brand, while financial profitability is based on luxury and premium product lines. However, as Kapferer (2015, p. 137) noted, the Dior case is unique in that its creative spirit is rooted in the *Griffe*, while the "bulk of its sales" come from accessories and premium brand product lines. Table 5.1 summarizes the revenue by divisions.

Marketing plays a different role in *Haute Couture* and ready-to-wear activities. An analysis of the CD marketing strategy can be made through the lens of the 4Ps. In terms of the product, marketing *Haute Couture* consists mainly of fostering a unique, iconic brand reputation in order to make the products highly desirable. This is supported by creative and unique designs, and fascinating fashion shows. As for the ready-to-wear segment, the marketing challenge is to develop a strong interpersonal relationship with customers (based on high-service quality, service customization, outstanding customer experience), while maintaining a cost-effective/profitable approach. This drives the company to

Table 5.1 Dior revenues by divisions

	Christian Dior Couture Haute couture, ready-to-wear, leatherworks and jeweler		Parfum Christian Dior Make up, skin care, perfumes	
	Turnover k €	Profitability k €	Turnover k €	Profitability k €
2017	1,142,709	63,992	1,629,171	208,994
2016	1,027,032	51,438	1,394,923	258,295
2015	975,263	37,144	1,348,619	196,797

Source Registry of the Courts of Commerce available on DIANE + data base

develop high-quality products, through craftsman-like, virtually "handmade" manufacturing processes, together with a high investment in the interaction between staff and clients.

For a longstanding brand as Dior, the challenge is to remain a desirable brand for young generations, while preserving the heritage and the excellence of the product designs. For this reason, the brand needs to be promoted with an emphasis on its history and DNA. As Sidney Toledano, Dior CEO from 2007 to 2017, explained in 2004, "Far from changing Dior's strategy in order to bow to the desires of younger consumers, it's the brand's heritage and authenticity that enable it to appeal to consumers of all ages in China and elsewhere. Luxury and fashion brands have to see what the new generation is thinking, but not by adapting and changing the products, philosophy and values because of the young generation; that would be a mistake" (Devilliers, 2004). This is a huge challenge for Dior given that young consumers represented 68% of its luxury sales in 2017 (38% for the X generation and 30% for generation Y). The relatively young age of CD clients is due to the rise in Asian demand.

Another challenge for *Dior Haute Couture* is to win over new targets. With this in mind, Dior recently began targeting men with high incomes. In this context, the promotion strategy is closely linked to the artification process, thereby justifying prices that are totally disconnected from the intrinsic value of the products sold by the brand. As Kapferer (2014, pp. 375–376) states "Although a handbag remains a bag, as a piece of art, its price must be totally independent of its function. (…) The artist endows the object with timelessness, substance, and cultural and temporal thickness."

For its adult ready-to-wear lines, CD outsources production to French and foreign manufacturers. The retailing strategy (place) is also central to this challenge. CD has developed an international network of shops and owns 198 retail outlets around the world. Their own stores generate 90% of sales. In Paris, the company owns the iconic Dior head office building, located at the prestigious address of *30 Avenue Montaigne*, where the story began. Other flagship buildings can be found in Hong Kong, Singapore, Shanghai, Seoul, Düsseldorf, London, Berlin, Miami, and New York. This strategy fosters the development of unique customer/brand relationships. In addition, Dior items are sold in some department stores. In July 2018, Christian Dior Couture opened a pop-up shop dedicated to its Autumn–Winter 2018–2019 collection in Harrods Luxury Store in London. Corners in airports are also a major source of revenue for luxury brands in general, and Dior in particular. They help to capture international customers and, as shown in a recent study, 18% of personal luxury sales are made in airports and small outlets (McKinsey Company, 2017). Finally, Dior has begun to take advantage of online retail (9% of luxury sales are made online). The recent advent of Jens Riewenherm, founder of the successful website mythereza.com, at the head of Dior's digital strategy marks a new stage in Dior's commitment to digitalization.

In order to better understand the key success factors of Dior and its links with art word, we have to turn to the company history.

Company History

The *Maison Christian Dior* was born in 1946 in Paris almost by accident. Indeed, Christian Dior was by no means predestinated for fashion. Born in 1905, in Granville, from a bourgeois family, he was attracted to the arts from a young age, but he eschewed studying the fine arts in order not to disappoint his parents and became a Political Studies student at the prestigious French *Sciences Po*, although he never graduated. In parallel, he continued nurturing his artistic interests, including contemporary music. A member of the Parisian art circles (Erik Satie, Jean Cocteau, Henri Sauguet were among his close friends), he opened two art galleries (in 1928 and 1932). There, he exhibited numerous major contemporary artists, including Salvador Dalí, Alberto Giacometti, Alexandre Calder, and even Picasso. Concurrently, he designed and sold fashion illustrations, some of which were published in newspapers such as Le Figaro. Noticed by Robert Piguet (1938–1940), he became one of his *couturiers* in 1938 and, in 1941, at the height of World War II, he joined the Lucien Lelong (1941–1946) fashion house where he worked as head designer along with Pierre Balmain. In 1945, CD met Marcel Boussac, the French textile tycoon, known as "the king of cotton" (Ottoni & Hudsick, 2013). Dior convinced Boussac to invest 60 million francs to found a new *Maison de haute couture* featuring his name, "where everything would be new, from the mindset and the staff to the furniture and the room" (Grumbach, 2008, p. 112).

The first collection, composed of 90 creations, was shown on 12 February 1947 in the heart of Paris, at Dior's legendary HQ at *30 Avenue Montaigne*, featuring his *Corolle* and *H-Line* silhouettes (Grumbach, 2008). "I drew women-flowers, soft shoulders, fine waists like liana and wide skirts like corolla" he explained. CD's sculptural skirts as well as the iconic "Bar" jacket were shown for the first time, subsequently becoming two major items of the brand for years after. The same day, the Editor-in-Chief of Harper's Bazar, Carmel Snow, wrote an enthusiastic article describing the work of CD as revolutionary and enthusing how his dresses "have such a new look!" (Dior.com). A correspondent from Reuters adopted the slogan, and very rapidly the newness perceived by the editor struck the world. Even if the *new look* was actually not the initial name of the collection, the press renamed it and made the new fashion company instantly famous. CD became a household name from one day to the next. In July of the same year, his collection flew to Sydney. In September, the American luxury department store chain, Neiman Marcus, gave him the prestigious Neiman Marcus fashion award. Newspapers at the time wrote "Unknown on February the 12th, 1947 and famous the 13th" (Grumbach, 2008, p. 114). The reasons for this tremendous success depend on the fact that CD was able to interpret what women were waiting for after the harsh war years. He marked the return to colorful, romantic, feminine and seductive dresses after years of strict and serious clothes (Grumbach, 2008, p. 114). During 10 years, CD launched twenty-two successful *Haute Couture* collections and became a part of the French couture scene. But, in 1957 he died suddenly in Italy.

His former assistant, Yves Saint Laurent, succeeded CD and triumphed with his first Dior collection ("Trapeze") presented in 1958. He left Christian Dior in 1960 when he was drafted into the army and Marc Bohan, former couturier for the London branch of Dior, replaced him. Bohan began an exclusive, almost thirty-year relationship with Christian Dior SA. He designed iconic dresses in keeping with CD's silhouettes and initiated fruitful cooperation with aristocratic families and the jet set, such as Princess Grace of Monaco (Okawa, 2007). During this period, the new shareholders are acquiring control of CD. In 1984, Bernard Arnaud (then CEO of Agache Willot group) invested in Boussac Group and became owner (among other brands) of Christian Dior SA (except the perfume branch, then property of LVMH group). In 1985, Bernard Arnaud became CEO of Christian Dior SA. For his part, Bernard Arnaud will continue his luxury brand's acquisition (he gradually acquires LVMH group from 1987 to 1989). These changes in financial property and governance result in changes in artistic Direction. Bohan is replaced by the Italian architect Gianfranco Ferré (arrived in 1989). For the first time, the artistic direction is held by a creator that has not been hired by CD himself. And this is a success. For his very first Dior collection, Ferré obtained the highest distinction in *Haute Couture*, the *Dé d'Or* or the Golden Dice award. With his personal vision of fashion and femininity, Gianfranco Ferré paid tribute to the style of Christian Dior creations. His work helped cement a new era of the iconography of the Maison Dior. Ferré instilled the "aura" of the Dior brand as a concept, a style, and a code (Fury, 2018). The company's activity definitively turned the founder, Christian Dior, into a creative genius.

In 1996, Bernard Arnault decided to initiate a sea change and put John Galliano in charge of the Maison Dior. As Antoine Arnault recalled, when his father made Galliano Dior's creative director "all the ladies of the Avenue Montaigne were outraged" (interviewed on French TV Show C'est à vous, France 5 TV, "*LVMH Antoine Arnault s'exprime*," 2018). However, the entrepreneur was right. The same year, Princess Diana arrived at the Met Gala dressed in a Dior model made by Galliano. From that moment, another myth took root. Under the artistic guidance of the British director, the brand entered a new era in which limits were pushed to the extreme (Kapferer & Bastien, 2012). For fifteen years, Dior challenged clichés as Galliano' creations were imbued with audacity and the desire to provoke. Galliano was summarily dismissed from Dior in 2011 after making anti-Semitic remarks and was blamed for an alleged assault in a bar in Paris. Evicted from the fashion house, the designer left a lasting legacy shaped by a taste for provocation, humor, and a genius for a Maison Christian Dior signature cut.

Former right-hand man of John Galliano, Bill Gaytten, temporarily took over until April 9, 2012, when the management announced the appointment of the Belgian designer Raf Simons as head of the Haute Couture, ready-to-wear and feminine accessories lines. Highly appreciated, his collections were characterized by minimalism and brought a new breath of life to the fashion house. Sales also took off again, but on October 22, 2015, Raf Simons announced he was stepping down to focus on his artistic career.

In July 2016, a new chapter opened with the advent of Maria Grazia Chiuri at the helm of Christian Dior. The first female artistic director had previously been the co-artistic director of Valentino. She invigorated the label with a magnetic modernity. With the dazzling success of a basic street style t-shirt showing the message *We Should All Be Feminists*, her debut Spring/Summer 2017 collection displayed the new director's strong conceptual signature. With reference to the political essay of Chimamanda Ngozi Adichie and perfectly timed with respect to the explosion of the "Me Too" feminist movement denouncing the exploitation and abuses of actresses in the Hollywood system, Maria Grazia Chiuri told the Guardian in 2017, "The Dior woman can be feminine in a strong way. I want to show [the women] behind my job. I'm not alone – in the atelier and in the archives, there are many women who work in the house. It's important to show what's inside."

CD history is not a long calm river, and its founder succeeded in just ten years of creations (and twenty-two *Haute Couture* collections) to establish the foundation of a unique brand. The next section highlights how artification sustains the success of the brand over time.

Artification Strategy

This section deals with the Dior artification process toward hybridization. Hybridization represents the strongest form of artification which, generally, can appear according to three forms of increasing intensity namely, synergies, contaminations and hybridizations (see Chapter 1).

In the case of Dior, hybridization emerged overtime through two mechanisms. The first one is the mechanism of heritagization i.e., actions consisting in giving a brand a heritage character (Davallon, 2006) and appears in two distinct strategies: (1) the celebration of the creator as an artist and, (2) the preservation of the Christian Dior heritage. The second one is the mechanism of spectacularization, and one can retrace it in how the brand makes it timelessly modern through fashion shows taking the form of unique happenings, and through the contemporary vision envisaged by extraordinary creative directors.

Heritagization Through the Celebration of the Creator as an Artist

To be artified, an object has to pass through numerous subprocesses (Shapiro 2019; Shapiro & Heinich, 2012) and among them, the recognition of the artistic status of the creator is essential (Shapiro, 2019). In the case of Dior, we identified a "celebration stage" where CD acquires the status of "artist." As previously mentioned, the history of Christian Dior is intrinsically linked to the art world.

CD had an art gallery and was a member of the Parisian artistic circles. Many of his collections were inspired by Cubism and Impressionism. Dior's creativity was undoubtedly influenced by the work of contemporary artists such as Marc Chagall and Bernard Buffet. Some of his dresses were even named after his artist friends, like the Braque and Matisse silhouettes in the Autumn–Winter 1949–1950 *Haute Couture* collection. This dialogue between artists was reciprocal, as they in turn painted his portrait (e.g., Bernard Buffet's portrait of Christian Dior). Beyond the death of creator, relationships with the art world also continued: "This permanent dialogue between art and fashion has continued long after the founding couturier's death through the talents of his successors" (Dior.com). Today the link with artistic circles appears as a brand signature. The CD creative directors loudly proclaimed their affiliation to art: from Jackson Pollock (Marc Bohan) to Picasso (John Galliano), from Degas to the surrealism of Magritte (Maria Grazia Chiuri). Certainly, works of art are displayed in flagship stores, with, first and foremost, the paintings of CD by Bernard Buffet (Dion & Arnould, 2011). This stage of

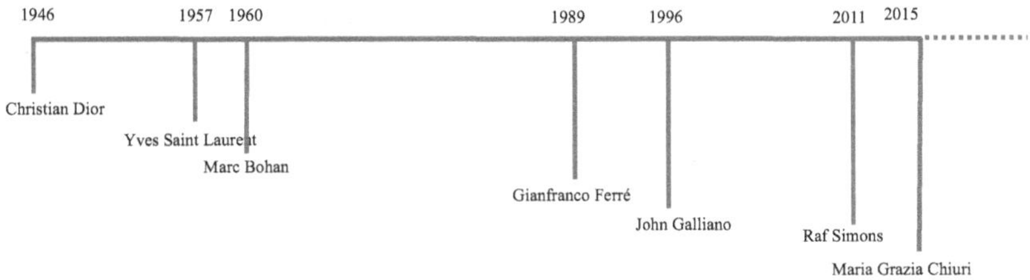

Fig. 5.1 Dior's artistic directors over time (*Source* Elaborated by the authors)

"synergies" between artworld and fashion brand is a basic form of artification (see Chapter 1) and is funded, in the case of Dior, on authentic roots.

What is unique in the CD case is the celebration of CD as an artist by the conservation of its "CD spirit" beyond its death. Yves Saint Laurent and Marc Bohan were hired by CD. They designed iconic dresses in keeping with CD's silhouettes and initiated fruitful cooperation with aristocratic families and the jet set, such as Princess Grace of Monaco. Later, Gianfranco Ferré paid tribute to the style of Christian Dior creations. His work helped cement a new era of the iconography of the Maison Dior. Ferré instilled the "aura" of the Dior brand as a concept, a style, and a code (Fury, 2018). The company's activity definitively turned the founder, Christian Dior, into a creative genius. Such strategies fit with what Davallon (2006) defines the heritagization i.e., the process of acquiring the symbolic status of "something to be kept" (Davallon, 2006, p. 2). Recently Maria Grazia Chiuri continues her work at Dior, presenting collections inspired by classical dancers and activists and following the Maison's heritagization process. Figure 5.1 shows the succession of the artistic directors over time.

The Heritagization of the Brand

Dior recently marked a turning point in the links between the fashion house and the art world by participating in many exhibitions dedicated to CD, its iconic collections and, more broadly, its "creative spirit," displayed across the globe. This is consistent with two subprocesses of artification. Following Shapiro and Heinich (2012) and Shapiro (2019) these are the *displacement* subprocess i.e., the fact to artify an object by taking it out of the contexts where it belongs to; and the *recategorization* i.e., the subprocess for which a previous "mere product" becomes an art object (see Chapter 1). Such steps of artification belong to the brand heritagization process (Davallon, 2006) which in the Dior case started *ante litteram* from the determination of members of the Dior family to keep the memory and legacy of Christian Dior alive. This determination took concrete form in 1987 with the *Christian Dior, The Other Himself* exhibition at the Richard Anacréon Modern Art Museum in Granville, France, curated by Florence Müller, which led to the founding of the Christian Dior collection. Ten years later, the Christian Dior Museum opened: at present the only French museum dedicated to a couturier. Since then, many fashion exhibitions have been held in museums, major heritage sites and art centers: Rodin Museum, Champs de Mars, and Grand Palais in Paris, Central Academy of Fine Arts and the Forbidden City in Beijing, Long Museum West Bund in Shanghai, etc.

In 2013, the MoCA, Museum of Contemporary Art of Shanghai opened the exhibition *Esprit Dior* with 100,000 visitors. Since then, the pace as well as the frequentation of exhibitions dedicated to CD has become even more intense. To celebrate the 70th anniversary of *Maison Dior*, a major exhibition was held in 2017 at the *Musée des Arts Décoratifs* in Paris (December 2017–January 2018). Organized by the same 1987 exhibition curator, Florence Müller, along with Museum Director, Olivier Gabet, the "*Christian Dior, couturier du rêve*" exhibition featured over 300 dresses, objects and paintings that had inspired CD, forming a comprehensive exhibition that enabled the public to discover the universe of the House of Dior's founder and the couturiers who succeeded him, from Yves Saint Laurent to Maria Grazia Chiuri. The exhibition welcomed 708,000[1] visitors in just six months and the queues were so long that opening hours were lengthened to nighttime in the last fortnight.

[1]This is a huge result for *the Musée des arts Décoratifs* whose previous record was 240,000 visitors for a retrospective on Barbie.

Personalities from the world of culture such as Florence Müller and Olivier Gabet played a key role in the brand's heritagization process, using TV and press conferences to propagate their expert views regarding the exhibition. Comparing CD to other twentieth-century artists such as Picasso, Olivier Gabet noted that there are three to five exhibitions a year in the world dedicated to Picasso, while the last exhibition dedicated to CD dated back to 1987. Moreover, the curators suggested that the Dior Group organize an exhibition not only to mark the anniversary of the fashion house, but also because Dior truly came from the world of art: "As an art gallery owner, Christian Dior was a man from the artworld, and the artworld went to fashion, not the opposite" (Gabet & Müller, 2017, p. 34). The role of the director is consistent with Kapferer's explanation (2015, p. 378) "To be credible, the process of Artification must involve the institutional actors of the art world. They are the ambassadors of luxury brands in this process." This is consistent with what Shapiro and Heinich (2012) and Shapiro (2019) defined as the subprocess of institutional and organizational change (see Chapter 1) of artification. Actually, the two curators give legitimacy (DiMaggio & Powell, 1983) to the artistic proposition made within the exhibits.

Another exhibition was organized in Australia, *Seventy Years of Haute Couture*. It displayed over 140 garments designed by *Christian Dior Couture* between 1947 and 2017. Yet another exhibition was held in the Denver Arts Museum, "*Dior: From Paris to the World.*" It featured 70 years of the *Maison Dior*, with a selection of over 200 haute couture dresses, accessories, costume jewelry, photographs, drawings, and other documentation that traced the history of the iconic fashion house. Maybe the best example of the success of the heritagization of CD is the exhibition that opened in February 2019 in London's famous Victoria and Albert Museum. The exhibition, "*Christian Dior: Designer of Dreams,*" celebrated the life and work of CD and his successors (Yves Saint Laurent, John Galliano, Raf Simons…) with more than 500 objects and pictures. In just a couple of days after its opening, the blockbuster exhibition had sold out, forcing the museum to extend the exhibition for seven weeks. This first exhibition dedicated to a fashion brand in the Victoria and Albert Museum beat the record for the largest number of visitors to a single exhibition (around 500,000 visitors).

These exhibitions and their popular success underscore the artistic nature of Christian Dior's work and, more generally, its key role in post-war fashion history. Iconic dresses that exemplify CD's New Look (e.g., the Bar jacket) are considered as authentic and unique pieces of art and as contemporary symbols of femininity. Table 5.2 reports a list of exhibitions and permanent collections dedicated to Christian Dior and to the Maison Dior since the'80s. From a theoretical viewpoint, the exhibitions clearly illustrate how "Extracting or displacing a production from its initial context is a prerequisite for Artification" (Shapiro & Heinich, 2012, p. 4). The artification strategy is now implemented in other Dior divisions. For example, since 2017, in the Dior's cosmetic division, the

Table 5.2 Dior's main temporary and permanent exhibitions

Place	Exhibition venue	Exhibition title	Year(s)
Granville (FR)	Richard Anacréon Modern Art Museum	*Christian Dior, The Other Himself*	1987
Granville (FR)	Christian Dior Museum	*Permanent Collection & Temporary Exhibitions*	1997
Shanghai (CH)	MOCA, Museum of Modern Art of Shanghai	*Esprit Dior*	2013
Paris (FR)	Musée des Arts Décoratifs	*Christian Dior, couturier du rêve*	2017–2018
Arles (FR)	Galerie du Cloître	*Dior, l'Art de la Couleur*	2017
Melbourne (Australia)	National Gallery of Victoria	*The house of Dior: Seventy Years of Haute Couture*	2017
Tokyo (Japan)	So-Cal Link Gallery	*L'art de la couleur. L'exposition*	2018
Denver (US)	Denver Arts Museum	*Dior: From Paris to the World*	2018–2019
London (UK)	Victoria and Albert Museum, London	*Christian Dior: Designer of Dreams*	2019
Dallas (US)	Dallas Museum of Art	*Dior: From Paris to the World*	2019

Source Elaborated by the authors

brand has launched an exhibition entitled Dior: The art of color to highlight the aesthetic universe of Dior, presenting the work of make-up artists such as Serge Lutens, Tyen and Peter Philips. This exhibition was first presented during the Arles photo festival, before going to Warsaw, Shanghai, Tokyo, and New York. In addition, the 2018 Dior exhibition, dedicated to the finest pieces of Dior jewelry and held in the Museum of Modern Art (Paris), highlights the artistic dimension of Dior jewelry creators.

The exhibitions are also indicative of the relationship that luxury has today with its archives. Beyond its success and its extraordinary nature, with the largest retrospective ever devoted to Dior, such events appear to exemplify the new interest in fashion houses for their own legacy. At the time of the first 1987 exhibition dedicated to CD, around 90% of the collection came from institutions other than LVMH, while in 2017, this percentage was reversed, and most of the Paris exhibition came from Dior's archives (Bosc, 2019). This trend can be found in the rest of the *Griffes* detained by LVMH Group. In fact, all the fashion houses now have their own Heritage Department. Concerning the Dior Heritage Department, it retrospectively purchases dresses, objects, and artwork linked to the founder and, prospectively, archives everything produced by the fashion house, in the same way as museums create and extend their collections over time. In addition, since 2011, LVMH has organized the so-called *Journées Particuliéres*, special days in which visitors are invited to discover heritage sites belonging to the Group, as well as visit the workshops and other places behind the production of LVMH's *Griffe* and luxury brands. This is done "*in order to showcase the savoir-faire and creativity of artisans, along with the architectural and cultural heritage of LVMH houses. To support an event inspired by generosity, openness and a desire to share exceptional places and creations with everyone*" (LVMH.com).

In sum, the heritagization process is the result of an ongoing strategy focused on maintaining and promoting Dior's legacy. It is developed both internally, with the Dior Heritage Department, and externally, through exhibitions and the *Journées Particulières*, as well as through other activities, such as the acquisition and opening to the public of CD's former houses. In particular, this orientation toward exhibitions represents a clear attempt of the company to displace CD work from the context of origin to a new institutional context, i.e., the museum. In this way, products can be recategorized as artworks as well as the designer can be recategorized as an artist (Shapiro, 2019). In this way, CD has managed to reinforce the timeless dimension attached to luxury products, which could be defined as the capacity to reach eternity, the certainty that the brand will still be there in 100 years (Wetlaufer, 2001). The age of a brand can prove its timeless nature, but Dior is relatively recent compared to "*grands crus*" or "champagnes," for instance. The preservation of Christian Dior dresses reinforces this timeless impression. However, by moving in this direction, the brand also runs the risks of "museification" (Lefebvre, 2015). The next point introduces how Dior overcomes this risk.

The Spectacularization of the Brand: The Creative Director's "Signature"

A last point contributing to CD artification process is the "abusive" starification of artistic designers placed at the head of collections (Dion & Arnould, 2011). The arrival of John Galliano has marked a turning point in this trend. We speak about "spectacularization of the brand" to highlight the efforts made by the brand to emphasis the creative talent and charisma of its art directors. We suggest that "spectacularization" helps the brand to lighten the risks of museification evoked earlier. At the same time, it shows how the hybridization between art and fashion is manifested through the expression of the artistic directors of the fashion house.

The creative directors who took over from Christian Dior undeniably helped to maintain the "spirit of the creator" after his death (e.g., Saint Laurent, Bohan). However, the creative directors gradually gained autonomous status with respect to the brand and its eponymous creator, bringing a breath of fresh air to the Couture Fashion House. The brand performance is largely due to the success of collections designed by creative directors such as John Galliano, Hedi Slimane, Raf Simons, and Maria Grazia Chiuri. All of them re-invented the CD "spirit" and made the brand more attractive. Obviously, John Galliano marked a turning point in Dior's modernization process (Kapferer & Bastien, 2012). The role played by the creative directors helps to keep the brand image contemporary and modern. In this way, the fashion designers nurture the artification process with the spectacularization of their collections.

Galliano, for instance, embodied the image of the "star designer" imbued with a strong personality (Kapferer, 2014). As Sidney Toledano explained "He knows how to create with each fashion show its own universe, with a vocabulary of its own and extremely strong visual references in order to be able to print a deep trace" (Devilliers, 2004). As already noted, Galliano modernized CD through provocation. We can trace his determination to shock with several examples. In 1999, he showed models dressed as tramps; the fragrance *Dior Addict* is deliberately associated with a drug, etc. However, Galliano was a master of tailoring and reinterpreted the CD classics, especially the *Bar* jacket, the emblem of the new look in 1947, reinventing it again in 2007 and again in 2009.

If John Galliano is a unique character (an extravagant British dandy), we could say the same for the following CD creative directors. Hedi Slimane was presented by CD as a young prodigy, a "dark," "rock," uncompromising and iconoclastic character. Maria Grazia Chiuri embodies a "feminist spirit" and offers Dior Couture House a new perception of women, incorporating political messages and committed to women's empowerment (De Garnier de Cassagnac & Berrebi, 2018).

The brand communication is largely built around the personalities of the creative directors. They are spokespersons for the brand on the Internet, in the press and, especially, during the fashion show season. Galliano, for instance, went up on stage at the end of his shows disguised in the theme of the collection. Toledano took note of this in an interview about Galliano and said, "He plays the game to the end: his salvation is expected as the final bouquet. It lasts a few minutes before appearing". Creative directors assume a special role for luxury brands. As Dion and Arnould (2011, p. 503) note, they have a "charismatic legitimacy" that is transferred to products and collections. Luxury brands, they explain, "have linked traditional legitimacy based on craft skills and know-how to charismatic legitimacy based on an exceptional charismatic persona, the artistic director who designs the products." As a consequence of hybridization, creative directors are considered as artists. In an interview with Suzy Wetlaufer on *Harvard Business Review* (2001, p. 118), Bernard Arnaud said about Galliano that "Artists must be completely unfettered by financial and commercial concerns, to do their best work. You don't manage John Galliano, the wildly iconoclastic head of the House of Dior, just as no one could have managed Leonardo da Vinci or Frank Lloyd Wright." The artistic status of creative directors is reinforced by their close relationship with the artistic community.

Further, all of the creative directors at Dior House are "art lovers" and some are recognized artists or art collectors. For example, Raf Simons worked with Sterling Ruby, an American artist, to design the Dior Men collection, is a friend of Marc Foxx (a famous gallery owner), and creates and collects works of art. In an interview, he explained "Of the top three or five things that are important to me, outside of family and love, art is No. 1. It's way more important than fashion. I keep thinking of things I would like to do that are not fashion. Making movies, making art — the practice of making something" (Fridman, 2018). It is a similar story with Hedi Slimane who is widely acknowledged as an artist-photographer (he has exhibited his work in the Foundation Pierre Bergé-Yves Saint Laurent, Paris) and whose work is largely inspired by music and art. Maria Grazia Chiuri also defends a commitment to female artists. She collaborated with artists when she worked at Valentino (Giosetta Fioroni) and she dedicates her fashion collections to artists who inspire her (Niki de Saint Phalle, Georgia O'Keeffe…) (De Garnier de Cassagnac & Berrebi, 2018). She initiated the *Dior Lady art project* in 2016, thereby expressing a close relationship with the art world. For the 2019 collection, she decided to ask 11 female artists to rework the already iconic Lady Dior handbag. These close links with the world of art blur the lines between creative directors and artists, leading to a vision of creative directors as "brand artists" (Dion & Arnould, 2011; Dion & De Boissieu, 2013). Since they are artists, creative directors "transgress prevailing aesthetic norms and regenerate them" (Dion & Arnould, 2011, p. 506), thereby providing the CD legacy with a new look. They also "sign" fashion collections and give artistic value to luxury products exactly as contemporary artists do with ready-made objects (Marcel Duchamp signed a urinal and transformed it into a piece of art). A typical example of this signature effect is that of the Dior t-shirt designed by Maria Grazia Chiuri. A feminist baseline "We should all be feminist" printed by the art director on a simple white t-shirt turned it into an "exceptional product" (priced €550, it rapidly sold out).

A second type of spectacularization has recently appeared in the form of the highly exclusive *Cruise shows*. Launched in 2016, CD was among the six prestigious brands to organize these extremely expensive mid-season collections. The *Cruise shows* are presented in May (between two seasons) to a "lucky few" in the form of a spectacular show. These recently established events in the luxury industry (15 € M for a show) target international shoppers and render the hybridization between art and the brand possible via a spectacular experience. For instance, CD organized cruises in the Californian desert in 2017 and in Marrakech in 2019. The event helps to celebrate the brand's strength and reinforces its iconic nature.

Thirdly, *Maison Christian Dior* is also a loyal sponsor of art institutions. It was the first sponsor of the New York Guggenheim annual gala (since 2013) and supports many art exhibitions, such as "*Contemporary Art in Versailles*" (Anish Kapoor's exhibition in 2015 and that of Oliafur Eliasson in 2016), *Bonnard* in the Paris Museum of Modern Art in 2006, and talent through the Dior Photography award for young talent. Even during the last Dior fashion show (2019), dancers from the *Mimbre Company* accompanied the models in a "circus" atmosphere to reinforce the artistic "happening" dimension of the CD fashion shows.

Finally, CD has initiated specific collaboration by asking contemporary artists to reinvent its iconic products. The brand commissioned famous artists such as David Lynch, Olivier Dahan, and John Cameron Mitchell to create a series of short films about "Lady Dior" (Macchi, 2013). Similarly, the "Lady Dior art program" involved established artists designing and exhibiting their own art-crafted, iconic Lady Dior handbags. Every year since 2016, famous contemporary sculptors, photographers, and painters have been invited to present their own version of this object. With the involvement of artists in the creative process as a consequence of the spectacularization of the brand, CD has entered the hybridization stage of the artification process.

Discussion and Implications

Christian Dior is part of a system that has dealt with profound changes in the world of luxury as well as in its ownership. Its success appears to be underpinned by the entrepreneurial roots that CD was able to develop in the 1950s. The brand was both innovative and visionary; not only in the style of its creations but also in its vision of the market, as licenses, "ready-to-wear" and its international appeal demonstrate. From 1947 to 1957, Christian Dior pioneered business units in the US (1948) and Venezuela (1952), developing licensing strategies (in Cuba, Canada, United Kingdom, and Mexico), and organizing fashion shows worldwide (e.g., in Brazil, Australia, Japan, Germany, etc.). This international expansion continued after his death and persists today.

The brand's acquisition by Bernard Arnaud in 1985 and its inclusion in the LVMH Group in 1989 marked a new era for the CD brand. The financial resources made available allowed the brand to reinvent itself. Today, it is recognized by consumers worldwide, reflecting a French lifestyle and a certain vision of femininity. The arrival of Maria Grazia Chiuri marks a new page in this history.

This chapter shows how the links between art and Dior over time have driven the brand's artification process, leading to hybridization. Indeed, the artistic nature of CD creations is now consolidated by exhibitions that take place in famous and highly reputed museums, including Victoria & Albert Museum or *Musée des Arts Décoratifs*. In the CD's case, artification takes the form of a hybridization through an extreme interaction between art and the commercial culture of fashion. The artistic nature of the CD brand makes it profitable by adding singular value to its ready-to-wear product lines. This hybrid form of artification transforms Dior products into art-inspired crafts and this is entirely in line with what foreign clients look for when they purchase luxury goods, namely, authenticity, French know-how and lifestyle values, historical and family roots. Lessons can thus be drawn about the artification of luxury brands from the CD case study.

First, we showed that in the CD case study, art is an authentic part of the brand's DNA. It appears to be a Dior specificity as opposed to other luxury brands that have created this link in a more artificial way.

For instance, the brand has penetrated certain Asian markets through the world of art, recalling the historical roots of the luxury brand and its authenticity (such as the first *Christian Dior and Chinese artists* exhibition organized in Beijing in 2009). The authentic relationship is highlighted in the content of the Dior Group's official communications as part of the brand storytelling, which draws attention to the close relations between Christian Dior and the major artists of his time (Marc Chagall, Bernard Buffet, Braque, Matisse …). We suggest that for hybridization processes to occur, they need to be rooted in authentic relationships with the art milieu, with blurred lines between art and fashion design.

Second, we highlight the importance of heritagization in the artification process (actions consisting in giving a brand an heritage character) to keep the brand's memory alive. The Heritage Department at Dior was one of the first to be opened by the LVMH Group, showing that Dior Group has always been *avant-garde* in exploiting its legacy. Sketches, production notebooks, catalogs, photos and press releases are preserved together with iconic garments, hats, shoes, bags, etc., to form a structured archive. This costly process involves developing new competencies similar to those required in museums. It is also a long-term process, taking over thirty years to collect CD pieces from around the globe and finding the ideal way to preserve garments. The lesson for luxury brands concerns how to organize and invest in the development of a heritage collection. This process can open the doors of international museums interested in exhibiting popular culture to attract new publics. In the case of Dior, we show that the link between the Dior brand and leading art institutions, such as the Victoria & Albert Museum, legitimizes Dior products, positioning them as somewhat superior to mere fashion items. Chanel, for example, followed a similar path with the *Mademoiselle Privé* exhibition, a retrospective into Coco Chanel's world, held in the Saatchi Gallery (London), West Bund Art Center (Shangai), and the D Museum (Seoul).

Third, the Dior case study shows the need to balance this historical approach to the brand with a modern and innovative perspective and we introduce the "spectacularization" stage undertaken in this sense. We highlighted the hybridization of creative directors who take on the role of artists to upgrade the historical vision of the brand, helping to avoid the risk of brand museification. Creative directors are able to refresh the brand image while retaining the *Maison*'s initial spirit. To this end, the heritage division developed in the Dior House which encourages brand directors to consult historical archives and to incorporate them into the brand's culture is particularly interesting. As we explain in this chapter, creative directors are considered as brand artists like Andy Warhol as explained by Schroeder (2005, p. 1294). They develop strong relations with contemporary art to instill a creative and innovative spirit into the brand. Creative directors are emblematic characters, associated with a powerful creative proposal and intrinsically linked to the art community. They are "leaders" that build "personas," inciting "adoration" and "devotion." An example of the capitalization of the artistic legacy left by the creators, including Christian Dior himself, is a series of books that Dior has published annually since 2016, dedicated to its seven iconic artistic directors. Following on from Christian Dior, Yves Saint Laurent, and Marc Bohan in December 2018, the fourth volume is dedicated to Dior by Gianfranco Ferré and highlights the precision of the cuts of the designer nicknamed the "fashion architect." In publishing one volume a year, these glossy volumes are similar to the art books we can find in art museums bookshops across the globe. We use the term "spectacularization" to outline the permanent show that has to be developed to keep the brand alive. In the case of Dior, spectacularization of the brand was initiated when Bernard Arnaud's LVMH group bought a stake of Dior House. The arrival of John Galliano as Dior's artistic director led to a total rejuvenation of the brand.

Dior was also one of the first fashion houses to invest in disruptive creative directors, a strategy that has since been emulated by other houses (e.g., Karl Lagerfeld revitalized the Coco Chanel Spirit). The Dior case study illustrates the balance needed between modernity and tradition. Spectacularization on its own would not be sufficient to "build" a luxury brand's artification. The "Lady Dior Art" project exemplifies this balance. Every year, famous contemporary sculptors, photographers and painters are invited to create their own vision of the "lady Dior" handbag, helping to make this simple handbag a "work of art." The choice of this product is not accidental. Lady Dior is a legendary product and the collaboration helps to reinforce this perception. Indeed, as noted on the website, in 1995, this iconic handbag become a timeless myth (…) and a symbol of the profound identity of the house. It embodies the spirit of the French fashion house as well as haute couture craftsmanship and know-how. The artistic collaboration highlights the timeless nature of Dior products (they are works of art, stamped with an artist's signature) and contributes to recognizing the artistic nature of the items and, ultimately, the entire brand product line.

Dior is an example of extreme level of interaction between arts and fashion i.e., hybridization. As it, other luxury brands might be inspired by this type of approach to sustainably establish their brand and avoid the pitfall of commoditization.

The case study demonstrates how, when a brand makes its journey toward artification, no difference persists between the brands' products and art, thus representing a strong potential as source of competitive advantage.

References

Bosc, E. (2019). *Les mémoires vives de la mode* (1re éd.). Paris: Les Echos.

Davallon, J. (2006). *Le don du patrimoine: Une approche communicationnelle de la Patrimonialisation* (1re éd.). Paris: Hermès Sciences Publications.

De Garnier de Cassagnac, A., & Berrebi, S. (2018). *The artification of fashion: A phenomenon transforming the discipline.* Retrieved February 6, 2020, from http://scriptiesonline.uba.uva.nl/cgi/b/bib/bib-idx?sid=3f7ae6f927494c58cc6c7b22318d769d;c=uvascript;type=simple;rgn1=keyword;q1=fashion;sort=publicationyear;cc=uvascript;view=reslist;fmt=long;page=reslist;start=5;size=1;lang=en.

Devilliers, S. (2004). Le PDG de Dior dévoile les secrets de sa communication. *Le figaro Economique,* 8–10.

DiMaggio P., & Powell W. (1983). The iron-cage revisited: Institutional isomorphism and collective rationality in organizational field. *American Sociological Review, 2*(April), 147–160.

Dion, D., & Arnould, E. (2011). Retail luxury strategy: Assembling charisma through art and magic. *Journal of Retailing, 87*(4), 502–520.

Dion, D., & De Boissieu, E. (2013). Construction et mise en scène d'un lignage dans le luxe: le cas des chefs dans la haute-cuisine. *Décisions Marketing, 70*(2), 25–42.

Fridman, V. (2018, September 25). Warhol & I. *New York Times.*

Fury, A. (2018). *Dior by Gianfranco Ferré.* Paris: Assouline.

Gabet, O., & Müller, F. (2017). Introduction. In F. Müller (Ed.), *Christian Dior, Designer of Dreams.* London: Thames and Hudson.

Grumbach, D. (2008). *Histoires de la mode.* Paris: Editions du Regard.

Jin, B., & Cedrola, E. (2017). Brands as core assets: Trends and challenges of branding in fashion business. In B. Jin & E. Cedrola (Eds.), *Fashion branding and communication: Core strategies of European luxury brand* (pp. 1–40). Berlin: Springer.

Kapferer, J. N. (2008). *The new strategic brand management: Creating and sustaining brand equity long term.* London: Kogan Page.

Kapferer, J. N. (2014). The artification of luxury: From artisans to artists. *Business Horizons, 57*(3), 371–380.

Kapferer, J. N. (2015). *Kapferer on luxury: How luxury brands can grow yet remain free.* London: Kogan Page.

Kapferer, J. N., & Bastien, V. (2012). *The luxury strategy.* London: Kogan-Page.

Lefebvre, V. (2015). *La museification des marques.* Retrieved February 6, 2020, from https://optiqueoblique.wordpress.com/2015/04/03/la-museification-des-marques/.

Macchi, J. (2013). *Lusso 2.0: nuovi paradigmi della comunicazione dei marchi di alta gamma.* Milano: Lupetti Editore.

MarketLine. (2017). *Christian Dior Strategy and Corporate Finance Report*, Progressive Digital Media Ltd. Ed., Retrieved February 6, 2020 from https://store.marketline.com/report/c9a67a81-ec7d-4499-9170-9050208405ae--christian-diorse-strategy-and-corporate-finance-report/.

McKinsey Company. (2017). *The State of Fashion 2017.* Retrieved February 6, 2020, from https://www.mckinsey.com/~/media/McKinsey/Industries/Retail/Our%20Insights/The%20state%20of%20fashion/The-state-of-fashion-2017-McK-BoF-report.ashx.

Michaud, D., & Masure, A. (2018). *La Haute couture et le prêt à porter de luxe. Etude conjoncture et prévisions.* Paris: Xerfi.

Okawa, T. (2007). La maison Christian Dior, modèle de référence pour les années 1960. In D. Veillon (Éd.), *La mode des sixties: L'entrée dans la modernité* (pp. 229–239). Paris: Autrement.

Ottoni, L. T., & Hudsick, M. (2013, August 22). *The new look: The introduction of a new body*. Retrieved February 6, 2020, from https://www.academia.edu/4924193/The_New_Look.

Schroeder, J. E. (2005). The artist and the brand. *European Journal of Marketing, 39*(11/12), 1291–1305.

Shapiro, R. (2004). *Qu'est-ce que l'artification?* XVII Congrès de l'Association internationale de sociologie de langue française, Tours, France.

Shapiro, R. (2019). Artification as process. *Cultural Sociology, 13*(3), 265–275.

Shapiro, R., & Heinich, N. (2012). When is artification? *Contemporary Aesthetics, 9*(4), 1–17.

Shapiro, R., & Heinich, N. (2015). *De L'Artification: Enquête sur le Passage à l'Art*. Paris: Editions de l'Ecole des Hautes Etudes en Sciences Sociales.

Wetlaufer, S. (2001, October). The perfect paradox of star brands. Interview of bernard arnaud from LVMH. *Harvard Business Review*. Retrieved February 6, 2020, from https://hbr.org/2001/10/the-perfect-paradox-of-star-brands-an-interview-with-bernard-arnault-of-lvmh.

6

Balenciaga: The Master of Haute Couture

Chiara Piancatelli, Piergiacomo Mion Dalle Carbonare, and Manuel Cuadrado-García

Abstract This chapter deals with Balenciaga, a brand that carries the name of the designer known as "The Master of Haute Couture", one of the most revered and influential fashion designers of the twentieth century. Characterized by sculptural quality, deft manipulation of textiles, and dramatic use of color and texture, Balenciaga creations are inspired by works of art and become works of art themselves through overlapping forms and genres. In this way, artification turns an elitist–but still commercial product—into a hybrid that acquires aesthetic and symbolic value and restores that aura lost due to production logics. Following

C. Piancatelli (✉) · P. M. D. Carbonare
Bocconi University, Milan, Italy
e-mail: chiara.piancatelli@sdabocconi.it

P. M. D. Carbonare
e-mail: piergiacomo.mion@sdabocconi.it

M. Cuadrado-García
University of Valencia, Valencia, Spain
e-mail: manuel.cuadrado@uv.es

M. Massi and A. Turrini (eds.), *The Artification of Luxury Fashion Brands*, Palgrave Studies in Practice: Global Fashion Brand Management,
https://doi.org/10.1007/978-3-030-26121-4_6

this perspective, the main contribution of the chapter is to highlight how Balenciaga developed hybridization processes since contemporary artists are involved in the creation of the new flavor of the Balenciaga brand. Through the analysis of primary and secondary data from different sources, the authors will also underline the relevance of luxury brands adopting this strategy that brings art and fashion to get innumerable mutual advantages. In conclusion, the authors draw main managerial implications.

Keywords Artification · Authenticity · Art · Balenciaga · Art & Brand Hybridizations · Luxury Fashion Brands

Introduction

Increased competition and market challenges, as well as the evolution of the consumer expectations and needs, pushed luxury fashion companies to identify innovative strategic approaches in order to succeed. The world of art and fashion could seem, in appearance, to be two antithetical realities: *art* is immortal, while *fashion* is transitory. Fashion is temporary by its very nature as it lives in the present, turning to the future with an eye always in the past (Marshall & Desborde, 2019).

The relationship between art and fashion, albeit often perceived as two worlds apart, is becoming increasingly indissoluble over years, nourished by the mutual collaboration and the innumerable advantages that both realities have drawn from it (Jelinek, 2018).

The management of fashion brands, especially in the luxury field, more and more occurs through a process of artification (Baumgarth, 2018; Kapferer, 2014; Kastner, 2013): in this perspective, Balenciaga represents an instance of the hybridization of art and fashion—fashion objects that become artwork. One of the first examples of collaboration between these two worlds is that of the Italian designer Elsa Schiaparelli, who lived in avant-garde circles of the 30s in Paris. Together with Salvador Dalí, she created surreal-looking dresses with lobsters painted on organza or velvet bags in the shape of a telephone. In his wake, in 1965 the master Yves Saint Laurent created the "Mondrian Look" inspired by the paintings of Piet Mondrian, inventor of neoplasticism. From the very beginning, Gianni Versace's most modern clothes were contaminated by the art world. The designer collaborated extensively with major contemporary artists, from Pomodoro to Veronesi, also creating clothes inspired by the art of Andy Warhol. In February 1982, the art magazine Artforum dedicated the cover to a dress of the Japanese Issey Miyake, celebrated as a work of art.

Building on the literature on artification—the "transformation from non-art to something art-like" (Kapferer, 2015; Naukkarinen, 2012, p. 63)—and authenticity (Kapferer, 2015; Trilling, 1972)—this chapter analyzes the case of Balenciaga, a brand that carries the name of the designer known as "The Master of Haute Couture," one of the most revered and influential fashion designers of the twentieth century, and emphasizes its creations through the arts experience. However, the shift from the sale of a garment to its exhibition as "a real work of art," a process now integrated into the most important museums in the world, was not as easy it seems. In their analysis of the relationship between art and fashion, Chevalier and Mazzalovo (2012), stated that before becoming one identity with two souls, the brand had to face a long journey.

Traditionally associated with exclusivity, status and quality, from a marketing point of view, luxury brands have interesting implications for the natural evolution of the luxury dimension (Kapferer, 2015). One piece of evidence: By promoting their products as a form of art and presenting their designers as artists, luxury fashion businesses are able to provide their brands with an allure of authenticity (Carù, Ostillio, & Leone, 2017). The example of Prada, which in collaboration with the duo Elmgreen and Dragset created the permanent installation Prada Marfa, located on Highway 90 in the middle of the Texan desert, is a demonstration of how art brings to fashion aura, status, and distinctive character. This strategy has allowed the brand to settle in a niche market, where the collaboration of a fashion designer with an artist fully legitimizes its work: the product takes on the appearance of a true work of art and can reach even a more distant target of customers engaged through the curiosity to know more about these new forms of collaborations.

Furthermore, art has a vital spirit that nothing else can equal and such a strong identity value that it is able to increase the power of a brand, improving the overall corporate image and guaranteeing both a good positioning and a stable financial situation (Kastner, 2013; Jelinek, 2018; Joy, Wang, Chan, Sherry, & Cui, 2014). A positive image return creates a universe of meanings around the brand that influences consumers to prefer it during purchase decisions. The Cristóbal Balenciaga Museum is one of the most deeply rooted examples of this reasoning, as it intends to celebrate the creative inspiration of the great Spanish couturier.

As suggested in the introductory chapter of this book, the reader is accompanied in several chapters with a framework of reference that explains, using a continuum, how art and fashion brands can interact strategically at different levels. In this chapter, we specifically explore the hybridizations strategy that Balenciaga undertook from a business point of view. With the term hybridization, the chapter points to a collaboration process among companies belonging to fashion and art sectors that decide to undertake a strategy aimed at creating a unique and authentic product/service in order to standout among competitors (Kastner, 2013; Jelinek, 2018; Joy et al., 2014). Being the realities considered those of the world of luxury and arts, the process of artification should be first taken into consideration as it allows the object to be perceived as an authentic and unique artwork. Artification strategies based on hybridization can be employed "at different levels of brand strategy: from communication to product design to retail sites" (Vukadin, Lemoine, & Badot, 2016, p. 278). Specifically, with the case of Balenciaga, the authors will argue that hybridization occurs when artists have an active role in the development, management, and positioning of a brand, while been faithful to their heritage and create entry barriers to competitor brands.

Consequently, the hybridization process—which represents an extreme level of interaction between the worlds of fashion and art, implying the intersection of forms and genres, generating grafts between high culture and commercial culture (e.g., a Vuitton bag designed by Murakami)—will be discussed in the case of Balenciaga through the analysis of primary and secondary data that were gathered from different sources: a semi-structured interview with the top management of Balenciaga, trade, academic journals, and newspapers, as well as from company documents such as annual reports, annual financial statements, industry research, corporate websites, and social media.

The chapter is organized as follows. First, a general overview of the company and the history of the Balenciaga brand will be provided. Second, the hybridization process between art and fashion will be dealt with through the Balenciaga case study. Finally, some managerial implications and main conclusions will be presented.

Company Overview

Renowned for its masterful cuts and construction techniques as well as constant innovation in fabrics, the Maison Balenciaga occupies a unique place in the world of fashion. The Balenciaga brand is a natural example of hybridization that implies the application of the "luxury is art" model (Okonkwo, 2007) or "art strategy" (Kapferer, 2014) on its business model. Balenciaga's hybridization brings the company to position itself at the extreme of the continuum presented in Chapter 1, where art and luxury become a single soul in a unique and authentic product (Jelinek, 2018) and where distinctive traits coming from the worlds of fashion and arts are mixed together. Through the overview of the success and impacts of the founder and the development of the company over the years, the chapter analyzes how hybridization strategies have ensured the development and success of the company. In fact, Balenciaga represents one of the most innovative fashion brands since its founding, applying artification and positioning itself as the Master of Haute Couture, while the relaunch of the brand has been characterized by a strong and well-managed hybridization strategy.

Founded in 1917 by Cristóbal Balenciaga, the company had a decisive influence on key haute couture trends. Since 2001 it has been part of the Kering Group, a global luxury group based in Paris that manages the development of a series of renowned houses in fashion, leather goods, jewelry, and watches. Since its foundation in 1963, the Kering Group has continually evolved and grown so that today it owns and manages brands such as Gucci, Saint Laurent, Bottega Veneta, Alexander McQueen, Brioni, Boucheron, Pomellato, Dodo, Qeelin, Ulysse Nardin, Girard-Perregaux, and Kering Eyewear. In 2018, the Group achieved revenue of €13.7 billion (Kering, 2019) (Fig. 6.1).

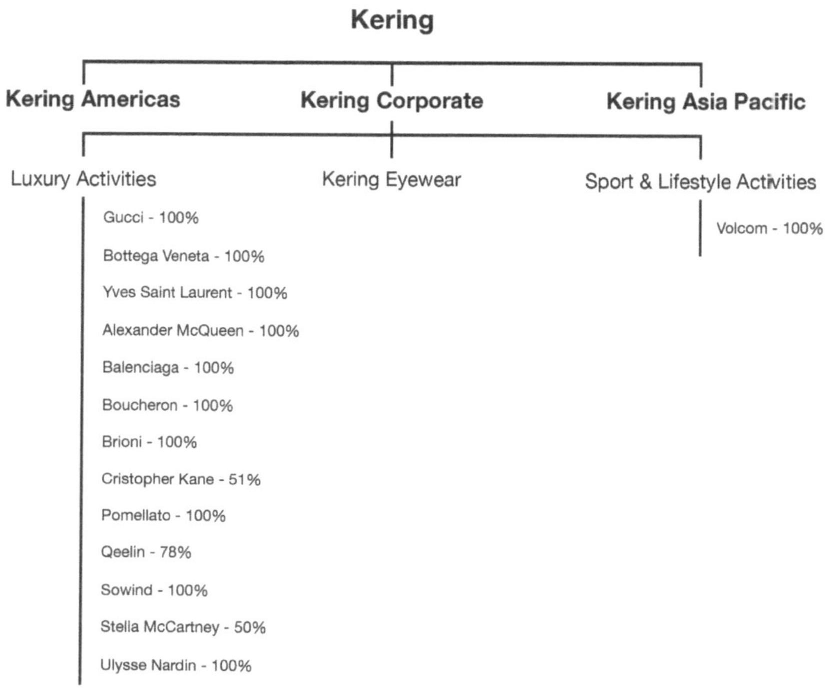

Fig. 6.1 Kering Group simplified organizational chart (*Source* Kering)

The luxury industry, including both luxury goods and experiences, grew 5% in 2018 to an estimated 1.2 trillion euros globally (Bain & Company, 2019). Mainly led by luxury cars, luxury hospitality, and personal luxury goods, which together account for more than 80% of the total market. However, varying economic trends, rapid digital transformation, and evolving consumer preferences are creating a new competitive landscape that threatens traditional corporate strategies (Bain & Company, 2019).

The report (Bain & Company, 2019) also points out the changes that this sector has been facing over the past two decades. The importance of the Chinese market (which accounted for 33% of the global luxury spending in 2018—the growth driven by local consumption rather than purchases by tourists), the continuous increase of the online shopping (10% of all luxury sales), and the critical influence of younger consumers on the overall success of luxury brands, represent the most significant trends identified in the report. The same source mentions that Generations Y and Z accounted for 47% of luxury consumers in 2018 and 33% of luxury purchases. In particular, the contributions of these younger generations to the market's growth are nearly 100%, showing that they represent the main target for the growth of luxury brands. Luxury companies are acknowledging this trend and have been challenged to meet the preferences of younger consumers in terms of product offerings, communication and engagement strategies, and distribution channels.

In 2017, Balenciaga had an operating revenue of 476.9 million euros and counts 822 employees worldwide (Orbis, 2019). Being one of the most popular luxury fashion brands, Balenciaga provides not only clothing but also accessories, shoes, jewelry, sunglasses, and other apparel that the company sells worldwide through two main marketing channels: physical and online stores.

Since 2013, Balenciaga has grown its revenues by 40% and its employees by 18% and most importantly the Maison was able to generate positive cash flows and net income (Table 6.1), representing the fastest growing brand in terms of turnover in the Kering Group in 2018 (Kering, 2019).

In recent years, Balenciaga has been consolidating its directly operated store network worldwide. Today, the House has a network of 156 stores in both mature markets (Western Europe, the United States, and Japan) and Asia (Greater China and South Korea). Balenciaga is also distributed through franchises and in leading multi-brand stores (Kering, 2018).

In 2018, Balenciaga pursued its retail expansion strategy with several net openings, including its first store in Miami's Design District and the takeover of franchise stores in Southeast Asia and the United Arab Emirates. Over that year, Balenciaga renovated a number of stores and the brand also extended its retail presence in upscale department stores with the opening of new shop-in-shops in Europe and Asia (Kering, 2018).

The online store Balenciaga.com confirmed its position in 2018 as one of Balenciaga's top-performing directly operated stores, and traffic continued to increase strongly. All regions enjoy outstanding results and the web experience aligns perfectly with the brand's audience and their shopping preferences. Mobile continues to be the preferred method for both

Table 6.1 Balenciaga financials—2013/2017

	31 December 2013 USD	31 December 2014 USD	31 December 2015 USD	31 December 2016 USD	31 December 2017 USD
Operating revenue (Turnover)	328,359,000	331,231,000	335,682,000	346,973,000	476,925,000
Net income	6,294,328	−4,738,394	−8,597,049	7,802,914	14,278,536
Number of employees	704	730	751	n.a.	822

Source Orbis (2019)

browsing and shopping. Today there are nine local versions of Balenciaga.com in different languages, including Chinese, Korean, and Russian. The Balenciaga website is e-commerce enabled in nearly 100 markets, such as the Middle East, South Korea, and China.

According to Cedric Charbit, CEO of Balenciaga, one of the key factors in the success of Balenciaga over the past few years is a new generation of clients who are more experimental—and far more impatient for new stuff (Ellison, 2018). More than 65% of Balenciaga's customers in 2017 were Millennials, accounting for more than 50% of their sales (Ellison, 2018). This trend correlates with the emerging traits of consumption characterizing the luxury fashion industry, which has increasingly become a source of enjoyment rather than being accessible and is frequently seen by people as self-reward (Doran, 2013).

In 2015, the arrival of Demna Gvasalia as Artistic Director opened a new chapter in the history of Balenciaga. The designer has deftly transposed the DNA of the Maison to cater to new customer expectations (Kering, 2017). Gvasalia considers Cristóbal Balenciaga's interest and ability as values when dressing a woman: to make her look or feel better in her clothes (Ellison, 2018). The ability to make women feel part of the product represents the added value of Balenciaga. Thus, the Maison does not work on trends, but considers that customers are going to wear the products, in order to link the "modern Balenciaga" to the heritage of this Maison (Ellison, 2018). With a masterful approach to volume and a deep understanding of technique, Gvasalia constantly pushes boundaries, blending streetwear and couture to reinvent a practical and contemporary wardrobe. Gvasalia's ultrarealistic and radical proposals for the Maison Balenciaga have won over a new generation of customers that is avid for novelty and authenticity. In 2017, propelled by its new creative momentum, the company enjoyed sharp acceleration and record performances. Based on the Lyst Index (2018), an analysis tool that tracks the shopping habits of 65 million consumers and 12,000 brands globally, Balenciaga ranked first (ahead of Gucci) in 2017 and has kept a stable third position in 2018 (Lyst, 2018). Balenciaga also opened its first flagship on the Avenue Montaigne in Paris, which reflects Gvasalia's newly defined brand concept. Lastly, the ramp-up of Balenciaga.com, an experience that aligns perfectly with the Maison's customers' expectations, resulted in a strong increase in e-commerce sales.

With such strong foundations, the Maison enjoys considerable growth potential, particularly in leather goods and accessories. Balenciaga's revenues, as stated by Mr. Charbit, are incorporated within the Kering portfolio of fashion brands, alongside Stella McCartney and Christopher Kane, but the luxury brand is on track for a billion mid-term (Ellison, 2018). Propelled by this impulse, Balenciaga is committed to developing its global distribution network, both physical and digital. In 2018, Balenciaga opened and renovated several boutiques based on a concept developed by Demna Gvasalia. In addition, Gvasalia defined the brand's creative expression in the digital realm on social networks and via an e-commerce platform available in over 97 countries (Kering, 2018).

Lastly, it is worth highlighting Balenciaga's social commitment. The company partners with the World Food Program (WFP) to raise public awareness of the growing global hunger crisis and support the organization's effort to eradicate hunger by 2030. The Fall/Winter 2018 collection, presented during Paris Fashion Week, included a selection of pieces with the WFP logo and, in some cases, the organization's slogan, "Saving Lives, Changing Lives." Every product sold provides tangible and concrete support to this program. Cause-related marketing is then undertaken, as contributions to the WFP comes from the sale of each branded product. Besides, that amount will be added to the $250,000 donated by Balenciaga to aid in the worldwide fight against hunger (Kering, 2019).

Thus, the following section will examine the figure of Cristóbal Balenciaga, his devotion to couture, and the subsequent development of the Maison since its foundation until today, highlighting the most important traits and also relevant events in its history, tracing the roots of its success.

Company History

Cristóbal Balenciaga was born in 1895 in Guetaria, a fishing village of the northern Vasque Country in Spain. His father, a fisherman, died when he was eleven-years old. His mother took the charge of the domestic economy, dedicating herself to sewing to raise her family. This fact allowed Cristóbal to be familiar with tailoring and sewing from a very early age (Vogue, 2018). After the outbreak of the Spanish Civil War, Balenciaga went into exile in Paris, opening his own design atelier in 1937. At that time, he presented his first collection with an outstanding success, becoming a famous fashion designer years later. His creations, based on comfort, purity of lines, reinterpretation of the Spanish tradition, perfection of fit, and development of volumes influenced fashion for three decades.

From that beginning in 1937 to the closing of the House of Balenciaga in 1968, he created some of the most outstanding and innovative examples of French and Spanish haute couture of the era, as Walker (2006), director and curator of the Texas Fashion Collection at the University of North Texas, notes. According to Walker, the internationalization of the Balenciaga firm, also located in Madrid and Barcelona, allowed him to reach a wider clientèle, including European aristocrats and Hollywood stars. In May 1968, the designer decided to close down his prestigious business (Miller, 1993), and he returned to Spain where he died in 1972. His withdrawal, consequence, among other factors, of the start of the pret-a-porter fashion, shook a leading industry in France. This decision was in line with the reticent nature of the designer, who always shied away from popularity and rather focused on his artisanal work.

Many of Balenciaga designs were influenced by different Spanish traditions such as bullfighting, religious background and artistic heritage, and his passion for great masters of Spanish painting. He was influenced not only by Goya's depiction of *majos* and *majas* in their regional dress or the habits of monks by Zurbarán, as Roglán (2006) points out, but also by Velázquez and cubist works of art.

Not only did Balenciaga use art as a source of inspiration in his work, but he also implemented them to make his creations, as his words confirmed: "A couturier must be an architect for plans, a sculptor for forms, a painter for color, a musician for harmony and a philosopher in the sense of measurement" (Vogue, 2018). His words explain the essence of his actual collections, which reflect the iconic style that has always been its trademark, celebrated with temporary exhibitions in the world and consecrated in the Cristóbal Balenciaga Museoa in 2011.

To implement his art, Balenciaga surrounded himself with his devoted family, some of them were involved in the business, and close co-workers whom he shared his expertise. Among these assistants were Courrèges and Ungaro, who worked for years at the House of Balenciaga before establishing their own ateliers (Walker, 2006). But the real success of Balenciaga is linked to the way he managed his Maison, similarly to how designers like Christian Dior and Coco Chanel did, allowing him to consolidate a recognized luxury brand and establishing the fundamentals of the luxury industry. In this regard, according to Walker (2006), Balenciaga's continuous innovation, obsession for quality, international fame, and communication of image were key elements.

Thus, Balenciaga's works are part of the most prestigious collections and have been exhibited in the main museums of the world, from the Metropolitan of New York to the Tokyo Fashion Foundation. One significant example was the exhibition "Balencianga and his legacy: Haute Couture from the Texas Fashion Collection" at the Meadows Museum of Southern Methodist University (Dallas, USA). According to its director Roglán (2006), the exhibit represented "a foray into another frontier in the arts, that of the history of fashion and dress." The collection included more than 300 creations by Balenciaga and other relevant designers, highlighting how much he influenced his peers. All those works selected for the exhibition were considered artistic expressions of the highest quality and taste.

More recently, in 2017, the year of Maison Balenciaga centennial, the exhibition *Cristóbal Balenciaga, l'oeuvre au noir* at the Bourdelle Museum in Paris showcased the talent of the Spanish master. Meanwhile, in London, the Victoria and Albert Museum presented the Maison's iconic pieces from May 2017 to February 2018.

Since its acquisition by the Kering Group in 2001, Balenciaga has undergone major changes and challenges. The current success of the brand is due to a strategy that has been implemented over the years and currently yielding results (Kering, 2018). The company revamped the couture approach of its founder, launching the "new couture" and being inspired by the same radical approach its founder had 80 years ago. The ability of Gvasalia has been great in bringing back the uniqueness of Balenciaga's pieces, making the new collection a mix between a piece of art and a fashion object. In this way, customers felt like buying unique and extremely valuable objects (Ellison, 2018). The impact of the newest Balenciaga's collections has been great in the fashion industry, driving other brands to make similar designs and products.

Today, the 100-year-old brand Balenciaga has also seen a surge of growth thanks to its soaring popularity with Millennials, who account for around 60% of sales. With its new streetwear-inspired look, Balenciaga was Kering's fastest-growing brand in 2018 (European CEO, 2019). Overall, the strategy of Balenciaga has been quite clear: building exclusivity and excitement, through a "return to the origins" of the brand. The Artistic Director has been able to replicate the approach that made Balenciaga the "Master of Haute Couture" by giving to its piece and collection the unique traits of a piece of art and ensuring that owning one of those generates exclusivity.

Artification Strategy

Hybrids and hybridization are concepts that are often related to science. Within biology, a hybrid is defined as being a mixture of two different species that normally would not be able to unite. The result of this crossing is a new breed with similarities to its ancestry but also with some unique qualities. When talking about hybrids and hybridization in fashion, we are beginning to see examples of similar phenomena in which outfits or garments are mixtures and crossings of materials, forms of production, styles, time characteristics, and so on—all of which would normally not have been imagined in a union.

With a fragmented fashion scene and a mix of many different elements in regards to both production and fashion expressions, this chapter explores the role of art used as a strategic tool to create value by luxury and fashion brands and subsequently to illustrate how luxury brands can be perceived by consumers when art is embedded authentically (Jelinek, 2018). Despite fashion brands increasingly employing art strategically, the proximity between art and luxury, constantly feeding each other, has not yet found an adequate response in terms of research on the topic (e.g., Kastner, 2013; Jelinek, 2018; Joy et al., 2014). Through the case of Balenciaga, whose haute couture products are often regarded as art (Jelinek, 2018), this section aims to look into the novel paradigms emerged in the fashion sector such as "luxury is art" (Okonkwo, 2009), "art strategy" (Kapferer, 2015), and the "M(Art) World" (Joy et al., 2014) to discuss and formalize the main reasons of a growing number of intersections between these two complementary realities.

Defined as "The titan of fashion," "The only true couturier," "The sculptor tailor," "The haute couture architect" by Coco Chanel, Christian Dior, Hubert de Givenchy, and Oscar de La Renta respectively, Cristóbal Balenciaga has not only revolutionized the history of costume—undermining the concept of femininity and the female silhouette—but has brought fashion beyond its borders by creating works of art that flee classifications (BBC, 2017). The strong connection of the Balenciaga brand with the art world has always been one of its hallmarks. As Jelinek (2018) claimed, the implementation of art and design has been visible in various ways in luxury. One approach is represented by those designers who break the boundaries among architecture, design, and art, playing a dominant role in their own creative products. The brand Balenciaga, together with other brands such as Raf Simons, Helmut Lang, Martin Margiela, Alexander McQueen, and Viktor&Rolf, belongs to this category and for this reason, it is a clear example of hybridization. These brands use the opportunity to surprise the audience by offering a multi-sensory performance, often including the creation of a Museum, which exceeds expectations by deploying "a way to combine art, culture, provocation and fashion" (Kubler & Smith, 2013, 34). Alternately, other luxury brands such as Prada place art as a clear marketing strategy to upgrade the brand image by creating a competitive advantage (Kapferer, 2015) or to create a strong unique selling proposition (USP) through the involvement of "emotional communications" that the arts world facilitate (Mazzalovo, 2012).

In the words of its Artistic Director, Demna Gvasalia, the strategy was clear: "We need to build excitement and expectations in the customer. We decided to give buyers a maximum number of orders they can take, rather than a minimum one. Our strategy? Exclusivity builds excitement."

The immersive digital presentation created for the Spring–Summer 2019 Balenciaga Show in Paris confirms how this luxury brand presented its new creations in an environment that is itself a work of art. The current Balenciaga creative director Demna Gvasalia and the contemporary artist Jon Rafman, whose immersive work has referenced video games, virtual realities, and Google's Street View mapping project always attentive to the culture of new technologies created the set-up. In this way, the launch of the latest creations of this fashion house was thought to be done in LED screen tunnels of 2000 square meters. Illuminated by a cold bluish light and the classic computer screen that announces the presence of an error, the environment began to come alive accompanied by gloomy notes. The visually startling journey continued to reveal alien landscapes, calamitous ecosystems, and techno-fetishistic civilizations on the brink of collapse (Jacobs, 2018). The collaborative design, featuring site-specific music created by BFRND, was effectively an immersive video installation, an all-encompassing virtual dreamscape that transported viewers inside the artist's digital mind. "We wanted to create the idea of being inside somebody's digital mind," said Gvasalia, "Through technology, we can transport people into another reality" (Jacobs, 2018).

Instead of waiting for the viewers to disseminate the collection, Balenciaga reimagined the fashion show by placing the viewers directly inside the landscape. As Gvasalia told Vogue, "Fashion shows are for transporting people, otherwise there's no point. It was like working on a movie, getting people into another reality, so it stays as a memory" (Vogue, 2018).

Lastly, it is relevant to mention the important project which took place in 2011. The Cristóbal Balenciaga Museum was inaugurated in his hometown: a space of more than 9000 square meters in homage to one of the great fashionistas, where more than 1200 pieces are exhibited. Run by the Cristóbal Balenciaga Foundation, the Museum has the mission, "to promote, develop and publicize the enormous importance of the figure and work of the couturier Cristóbal Balenciaga Eizaguirre in the world of fashion and particularly haute couture, and in artistic creation in general" (Cristóbal Balenciaga Museoa, 2019). The importance of this

Museum is reflected in its Board of Trustees, the highest governing body of the Foundation, comprised by ex officio trustees (representatives of the Spanish Ministry of Culture, Basque Government, Provincial Council of Guipuzkoa, Guetaria town Council, and some appointed members), elected representatives (president and vice-president), and Honorary appointments (King and Queen of Spain).

This public institution, dedicated to conserving, researching, and transmitting the figure and work of fashion designer Cristóbal Balenciaga, continuously organizes exhibitions and programs related to the couturier and the world of fashion, housing one of the biggest collections of this famous creator's works. Specifically, the museum hosts a permanent collection with a classic but tasteful decoration and other temporary exhibitions related to the designer. Besides, as stated in its website, the Education Department is in charge of organizing and running educational and mediation activities "to provide visitors with access to knowledge and help them enjoy the items in museum's permanent and temporary exhibitions." These activities are adapted to different segments: schools, families, people with special needs, and people in danger of social exclusion. The Collections Department carries out intense research activity based on the exhaustive study and documentation of the Balenciaga creations belonging to its collection, as well as on obtaining greater knowledge of the personal and professional career of the couturier. All this work is later transmitted in exhibitions and publications.

The Museum also offers many different peripheral services such as guided and accessible tours, shops, resting area, cloakroom, information point, and auditorium to create greater value to customers, feeding among others, sartorial tourism, and an increasingly growing phenomenon. All this has made it possible that the name of Balenciaga continues to flourish today as that of a prominent international company. For Walker (2006), this sense of continuity and consistency was a hallmark of Balenciaga that can be found in his extant work around the world. Thus, the Balenciaga experience finds in its museum the place of consecration of the link between the art world and the world of luxury. This will be deepened by the authors as an example of hybridization between these two complementary worlds, specifically between fashion and art.

Furthermore, the Balenciaga brand is a natural example of hybridization that implies the application of the "luxury is art" model (Okonkwo, 2007) or "art strategy" (Kapferer, 2014) on its business model bringing the company to position itself at the extreme of the continuum presented in Chapter 1, where art and luxury become a single soul in a unique and authentic product (Jelinek, 2018) and where distinctive traits coming from the worlds of fashion and arts are mixed together. The identification and analysis of the effects that can occur in the hybridization between fashion and art, allow us to grasp the reasons why its actors choose to invade—in an authentic (as in the Balenciaga case) way—a contiguous field (Ellison, 2018).

Art is emotion, any other deterministic definition would be inadequate: luxury brands, through their creations, excite. Following this perspective and working together fashion and luxury are creating a magical universe (Jelinek, 2018).

Conclusion and Implications

The increasing competition and market challenges, as well as the evolution of the consumer expectations and needs, pushed luxury and fashion companies to identify innovative strategic approaches to succeed. In this context, as Jelinek (2018) suggests, the application of art, the collaboration with artists, and the implementation of experiential strategies lead to a competitive advantage and a sustained value creation for luxury brands.

The aestheticization of consumer experience along with the commodification of aesthetic experience has been characterizing the luxury market, pushing companies to include in their strategies elements related to function, behaviour, and aesthetics (Joy et al., 2014). As per the aesthetics, the relationship between luxury brands and art is recognized as a competitive advantage for the brand, however, this advantage is as such only when the relationship is able to preserve the true values of the luxury brand itself (Jelinek, 2018). In particular, the need to provide authentic and unique experiences to luxury consumers represents a key aspect of the success of the artification strategies adopted by luxury brands. In the case of Balenciaga, such authenticity is provided by connecting not only the products of the Maison but also its heritage and history, allowing consumers to be part of their own personal identities (Joy et al., 2014).

However, unlike partnership and sponsorship, which use the connection with the art to enhance the value of the brand and to shift it to an iconic status, the hybridization strategy allows companies to create unique products and experiences. These products and experiences represent the identity of the brand and are not simply seeking to increase their value and perceptions. By creating a unique experience in their fashion shows, Balenciaga's products become artworks and a "model for appreciation and reverence" (Dion & Arnould, 2011). Offering multi-sensory performances, which combine art, culture, provocation, and fashion, thus surprising the audience, represents a strategy to integrate art into the luxury industry. Such an approach, when applied by luxury fashion brands, ensures a competitive advantage in the originality of the product design and the perception of the consumer of the brand (Kubler & Smith, 2013).

Supporting the hybridization of art and fashion requires the acknowledgement of the heritage of the company as well as its respect as the story of the Balenciaga brand. In this sense, the role of the creative director of the company is critical. On one side, the person who covers this role should be able to fully interpret the values of the company and on the other side, he/she should also have a mid-term perspective. Ensuring that the creative director has the time and opportunities to absorb the values and interpret it through an authentic aesthetic experience is fundamental in such a strategy. Hence, hybridization's strategy must look at the long-term period, avoiding spot collaborations.

Another important aspect to be taken into consideration is the experience of the creative director. In this sense, that experience and seniority along with his/her understanding of the values of the brand, represents a win–win situation since his/her value and visibility will not be altered by that of the brand itself. The case of Balenciaga represents a positive example of how a strong Creative Director has been able to interpret and transfer the values of the company, leveraging on the heritage and originality of the founder.

Luxury brands are leveraging the power to engage and interest of the art world in order to attract customers and increase their loyalty. As is emerges in the case of Balenciaga, the brand allows consumers to live the unique aesthetic experience of visiting a museum or owning a piece of art. This brand's products are invested with the artistic concepts of skill, heritage, craftsmanship, and authenticity. Such hybridization represents an opportunity not only to provide an ultimate aesthetic experience, but also to transfer the heritage of the brand. In fact, consumers embrace not merely products, but also brand heritage and history (Joy et al., 2014).

The Cristóbal Balenciaga Museum in Guetaria (Spain) is a place where visitors can admire the legacy of the Master of Haute Couture and his pieces are treated as masterpieces by Caravaggio or Picasso. This generates a positive impact on the equity of the brand, increasing it and ensuring that the brand benefits from its art hybridization.

The fashion apparel becomes unique and full of significance thanks to the integration between the brand heritage, the creativity of the Creative Director, and the ability to transfer this uniqueness to the consumer. This approach exceeds consumers' expectations thanks to the combination of art, culture, provocation, and fashion (Kubler & Smith, 2013), generating higher value for the consumer itself and clearly positioning the brand.

Through the Balenciaga case, this chapter has shown how art has become central to the development and management of luxury brands. The collaborations and synergies promoted by the worlds of fashion and art aimed at generating unique and authentic products or services represent the deepest level of collaboration, which has proven to be a successful strategy for luxury brands.

Based on Balenciaga's values and the strategy of its Creative Director, luxury and fashion brands need to amaze consumers by demonstrating the authenticity of their products through an innovative journey that includes engaging consumers through the art experience. The multi-sensory performance of Balenciaga Spring–Summer 2019 fashion show installation represents an instance of this process—that reflects the original values of the company. In this perspective, the artistic experience makes the products unique and supports the development of consumer taste, which, as a consequence, drives consumption. The case of Balenciaga demonstrates how, through a hybridization process, fashion items, immersed in an art environment—designed by artists—become hybrids, a perfect blend of fashion and art.

By turning into artistic objects, luxury and fashion products become drivers of consumption and brand loyalty, thus representing a competitive advantage for the sustained value creation of luxury brands. In this context, hybridization represents a strategic tool for luxury brands to support their positioning in the luxury market.

Among the sources of competitive advantage for luxury brands are both managerial aspects—such as innovation, long-term investment, brand identity, and production-related aspects—such as the originality of the product and the heritage of the Company (Baker, 2007; Jackson & Shaw, 2009). Leveraging both aspects, luxury fashion brands are able to guarantee their competitive advantage while establishing an authentic relationship with the consumer through the uniqueness of the product and the experience produced by the arts world. The Balenciaga case highlights that hybridizations are collaborations characterized by an extreme level of interaction that implies the intersection of forms and genres, generating grafts between high culture and commercial culture.

References

Bain & Company. (2019). *The future of luxury: A look into tomorrow to understand today*. Retrieved February 13, 2019, from https://www.bain.com/contentassets/8df501b9f8d6442eba00040246c6b4f9/bain_digest__luxury_goods_worldwide_market_study_fall_winter_2018.pdf.

Baker, M. J. (2007). *Marketing strategy & management*. London: Palgrave Macmillan.

Baumgarth, C. (2018). Brand management and the world of the arts: Collaboration, co-operation, co-creation, and inspiration. *Journal of Product & Brand Management, 27*(3), 237–248.

BBC. (2017). *How luxury firms are using art to attract customers*. Retrieved February 13, 2019, from https://www.bbc.com/news/business-40592986.

Carù, A., Ostillio, M. C., & Leone, G. (2017). Corporate museums to enhance brand authenticity in luxury goods companies: The case of Salvatore Ferragamo. *International Journal of Arts Management, 19*(2), 340–362.

Chevalier, M., & Mazzalovo, G. (2012). *Luxury brand management: A world of privilege*. Singapore: Wiley.
Cristóbal Balenciaga Museoa. (2019). *Cristóbal Balenciaga Museoa*. Retrieved February 13, 2019, from https://www.cristobalbalenciagamuseoa.com.
Dion, D., & Arnould, E. (2011). Retail luxury strategy: Assembling charisma through art and magic. *Journal of Retailing, 87*(4), 502–520.
Doran, S. (2013). *The new luxury is luxury for all, suggests Jean-Noël Kapferer*. Retrieved February 13, 2019, from http://luxurysociety.com/articles/2013/04/the-new-luxury-isluxury-for-all-suggests-jean-noel-kapferer.
Ellison, J. (2018). *Balenciaga's billion-euro plan*. Retrieved February 13, 2019, from https://www.ft.com/content/b8da67b2-f09b-11e7-b220-857e26d1aca4.
European CEO. (2019). *François-Henri Pinault's refined approach brings Kering success*. Retrieved October 10, 2019, from https://www.europeanceo.com/profiles/francois-henri-pinaults-refined-approach-brings-kering-success/.
Jackson, T., & Shaw, D. (2009). *Mastering fashion marketing*. Basingstoke: Palgrave Macmillan.
Jacobs, L. (2018). *Balenciaga in Black Review: Fashion goes to the dark side*. Retrieved February 13, 2019, from https://www.wsj.com/articles/balenciaga-in-black-review-fashion-goes-to-the-dark-side-1539112816.
Jelinek, J. S. (2018). Art as strategic branding tool for luxury brands. *Journal of Product & Brand Management, 27*(3), 294–307.
Joy, A., Wang, J. J., Chan, T.-S., Sherry, J. F., Jr., & Cui, G. (2014). M(art) worlds: Consumer perceptions of how luxury brand stores become art institutions. *Journal of Retailing, 90*(3), 347–364.
Kapferer, J. N. (2014). The artification of luxury: From artisans to artists. *Business Horizons, 57*(3), 371–380.
Kapferer, J. N. (2015). *Kapferer on luxury: How luxury brands can grow yet remain rare*. London: Kogan Page.
Kastner, O. L. (2013). *When luxury meets art: Forms of collaboration between luxury brands and the arts*. London: Springer.
Kering. (2017). *Activity Report*. Retrieved February 13, 2019, from http://www.kering.com/activity-report-2017/text-to-speech/the-brands/balenciaga.html.
Kering. (2018). *Financial document*. Retrieved April 20, 2019, from https://www.kering.com/en/special-reports/finance.
Kering. (2019). *About Kering and key figures*. Retrieved April 20, 2019, from https://www.kering.com/en/finance/about-kering/.
Kubler, A., & Smith, M. O. (2013). *Art/fashion in the 21st century*. London: Thames & Hudson.

Lyst. (2018). *The Lyst index*. Retrieved February 13, 2019, from https://www.lyst.com/the-lyst-index/2018/q3/.
Marshall, K. P., & Desborde, R. (2019). *A proposal for fine arts market segmentation based on functions of art and consumer benefits sought*. Retrieved February 13, 2020, from https://digitalcommons.kennesaw.edu/cgi/viewcontent.cgi?article=1293&context=ama_proceedings.
Mazzalovo, G. (2012). *Brand aesthetics*. London: Springer.
Miller, L. E. (1993). *Cristóbal Balenciaga*. New York: Holmes & Meier.
Naukkarinen, O. (2012). Variations on artification. *Contemporary Aesthetics*, 4.
Okonkwo, U. (2007). *Luxury fashion branding—Trends, tactics, techniques*. New York: Palgrave Macmillan.
Okonkwo, U. (2009). The luxury brand strategy challenge. *Journal of Brand Management, 16*(5–6), 287–289.
Orbis. (2019). *Balenciaga*. Retrieved April 13, 2019, from https://orbis.bvdinfo.com.
Roglán, M. (2006). Foreword. In M. Walker, M. (Ed.), *Balenciaga and his legacy: Haute couture from the Texas Fashion Collection*. New Haven and London: Yale University Press.
Trilling, L. (1972). *Sincerity and authenticity*. Cambridge: Harvard University Press.
Vogue. (2018). *Balenciaga*. Retrieved February 13, 2019, from https://www.vogue.es/moda/modapedia/disenadores/cristobal-balenciaga/172.
Vukadin, A., Lemoine, J. F., & Badot, O. (2016). Opportunities and risks of combining shopping experience and artistic elements in the same store: A contribution to the magical functions of the point of sale. *Journal of Marketing Management, 32*(9–10), 944–964.
Walker, M. (2006). *Balenciaga and his legacy*. New Haven, CT: Yale University Press.

Index

M. Massi and A. Turrini (eds.), *The Artification of Luxury Fashion Brands*, Palgrave Studies in Practice: Global Fashion Brand Management, https://doi.org/10.1007/978-3-030-26121-4

FSC
www.fsc.org
MIX
Papier | Fördert
gute Waldnutzung
FSC® C083411

Kolibri 360 GmbH
Ferdinand-Jühlke-Straße 7
99095 Erfurt, Deutschland
produktsicherheit@kolibri360.de